TO REME
AND TO HEAL

TO REMEMBER AND TO HEAL

Theological and Psychological
Reflections on
Truth and Reconciliation

EDITED BY
H RUSSEL BOTMAN AND
ROBIN M PETERSEN

HUMAN & ROUSSEAU
Cape Town Pretoria Johannesburg

Contents

Foreword

The Truth and Reconciliation Commission has a clear political focus and strong legal implications. It is, at the same time, at its heart a deeply theological and ethical initiative. For people of faith, the experience of honesty and mercy, confession and forgiveness, justice and peace, repentance and reconciliation is what *truth and reconciliation are all about*.

I am delighted to be associated with this collection of essays edited by Russel Botman and Robin Petersen. The essays are a mixture of personal and, at times, agonising experiences, as well as reflection, analysis and sound theological thinking. I commend this book, not only to those inside the faith community, but to all people who share the desire to deal with the past in a creative way by telling the truth and working for reconciliation.

Storytelling is central, not only to the many religions practised in this country, but also to the African tradition of which we are a part. Ellen Kuzwayo is quoted in these essays as saying: "Africa is a place of storytelling. We need more stories never mind how painful the exercise might be. This is how we will learn to love one another. Stories help us to understand, to forgive and see things through someone else's eyes." These are wonderful words. They are fundamentally true. We also need theological and ethical resources to understand the stories that we hear. It is in relation to this need that the essays contained in this publication fulfil such an important role.

Our nation needs healing. Victims and survivors who bore the brunt of the apartheid system need healing. Perpetrators are, in their own way, victims of the apartheid system and they, too, need healing. Religion is central to this process of healing. We need to reach deep into the spiritual wells of our different religious traditions practised in this country in order to draw strength and grace with which to address the challenges of healing and nation building. Those of us who stand within the Christian tradition have, perhaps, a special responsibility in this regard because this nation has through the years employed Christian theological resources to promote apartheid – a system that is today accepted by people throughout the world as a crime against humanity.

My sincere hope is that this book will be read as widely as it deserves to be read and that the ideas contained between its pages will be appropriated by all South Africans.

THE MOST REVEREND DESMOND M TUTU
CAPE TOWN, JUNE 1996

H Russel Botman and Robin M Petersen

Introduction

The mother's voice cracked with the unbearable agony: "I found Bheki. He was in pieces. He was hanging on the curtains, he was all over, there were pieces of brains all over. That was the end of Bheki."

This was one of the many horrifying testimonies to the Truth and Reconciliation Commissioners. Catherine Mlangeni tells the story of the murder of her son Bheki Mlangeni. Next to her sits her daughter-in-law Sepati, the widow ... listening ... crying ... remembering. Mlangeni, a promising young Soweto lawyer, was blown to pieces by a booby-trapped tape player headset. Archbishop Desmond Tutu vicariously wipes a tear on behalf of the nation.

What is the truth? This is the unresolved question between Jesus and Pontius Pilate. John 18:38 says that Pontius Pilate immediately left the interrogation room after his rhetorical question. To Pilate it represented an insoluble question of legal justice. Jesus, on the other hand, sees that witnessing to the truth is more than what courts of laws can do. It appears that truth possesses a powerful force which is able to divide people between those who turn it into a matter of theory and those who turn it into an issue of praxis (witnessing). This book is written in an attempt to go beyond the merely theoretical and yet remain faithful to the necessary tension between theory and praxis in the issue of national reconciliation.

South African newspapers report the many stories as best they can. The more they report the less the occurrence of the word *reconciliation*. Afrikaans establishment newspapers speak degradingly of the "Biegkommissie" (confessing commission) or "Biegbank" (confessing court) derived from "regbank" (court of justice) while English-language newspapers more often than not simply refer to the "Truth Commission". This book is a reminder that we have before us more than we could imagine. As a nation we are confronting the demons of our past to exorcise them so that we may build the kind of community reconciled to face the future. It is about confession, but not only that. It is also about the truth, but it is much more than that as well. The crux of it all is how these things hold together in the interest of national reconciliation.

Facing these harrowing realities the people of South Africa have resolved to remember and constructively "master the past", to show contriteness, to confess, to forgive, to reconcile. This book struggles with the real meaning of reconciliation as a national process and a national asset, not only the self-serving interest of some or other group.

The first weeks of the hearings have been overshadowed by the restrictive nature of impending and executed court orders. Bomb threats have also disrupted the proceedings. Perpetrators and victims alike have a love-hate relationship with the Commission. Perpetrators want a Commission that can help them "and the nation" to put the past behind them and get on with the future, but they are reluctant to come forward to testify. Victims want the dignity of their loved ones restored, their remains properly buried, and the nation to have an indelible memory of what has happened in this country in the name of a Christian government, but they remain ambivalent about the granting of amnesty to perpetrators.

Painfully, we are becoming aware of the need to understand the very difficult relationship between reconciliation and justice. For some people these notions are synonymous. To others they are mutually exclusive. This book assumes that although truth and reconciliation relate directly to each other, reconciliation is neither synonymous with nor exclusive of justice. Reconciliation is not meant to subvert justice but neither does it replace it. The many stories that we hear about the difficulties with the Nuremberg trials warn us against a simplistic connection between reconciliation and justice. These trials, as well as the Stasi-investigations in the former East Germany, show how difficult the issue of legal justice aimed at the perpetrators can become. In so many instances the courts could not conclusively rule against alleged perpetrators and many victims were frustrated and felt more humiliated by the process. The triumphalism of those who stood by the alleged perpetrators did not ease the pain of the victims.

The South African attempt to negotiate these competing demands is not in the first place aimed at the perpetrator. Its immediate focus is the restoration of the humanity and dignity of the victim. The Commission is an instrument of the State briefed to do just that. The country has decided to put its energy into the project of restoring the humanity and dignity of the victim. This is precisely what draws the tears from the eyes of Archbishop Tutu and many of us: we have an opportunity to tell and to participate in each other's horrifying stories so that we can share in a new common humanity born of pain and suffering. Reconciliation neither replaces nor excludes legal justice. However, it is also unacceptable to make it posterior to the satisfaction of the legal requirements of justice. Reconciliation builds the foundation of commonality which makes it possible for justice to be done in the spirit of openness and acceptance of the other and in the interest of our common future. Reconciliation replaces the culture of revenge, not the culture of justice.

Nor does reconciliation preclude compensation and reparation. It is in the nature of confession that the confessed wrong be redressed. Many victims tell more than just horrific stories of physical and psychological violence, they also tell of the ongoing effects of this horror on the survivors and their families. The cost that has been exacted from them continues to be paid. Reparation is but a necessary, albeit first, step to healing and reconciliation.

The work of the TRC is made enormously difficult by the constitutional clause on "amnesty". It creates an unnatural cohabitation of reconciliation and legal justice which is difficult if not impossible to defend on religious grounds. However, it may well have to be embraced on practical grounds. It clearly was a political trade-off, and in that sense it is the price victims will be paying for the kind of political settlement that was attainable.

Except for one letter from an unnamed Afrikaans dominee and the statements and tears of Archbishop Tutu we have seen, to date, very little of the response of the religious community to this profound challenge. Although there have been many things happening among the churches at a regional level, there has been little systematic reflection on the theological, moral and religious questions that the TRC process raises for the churches. This is somewhat surprising, given that the notions of "truth" and "reconciliation" lie at the heart of at least the Christian tradition, and are a central part of others as well. This book is an attempt to provide some of those resources and reflections.

We begin with a story. It is the story of Father Michael Lapsley, victim of a horrific letter bomb which he received after the release of Nelson Mandela and the unbanning of the liberation movements. His powerful story sets the scene for the book, for if the first days of hearings of the TRC have shown us anything, it is that the telling of stories is central to the process. It is the stories that we have heard and will continue to hear that make the process so compelling. For in listening to stories we encounter people, the people whose names, familiar and unknown, had sometimes been reduced to ciphers of the struggle, symbols which evoked much (the tragic litany of Biko, Timol, Mohaphi, Aggett, Webster, Goniwe, Calata, Heyns and many many more) but at the same time concealed a whole world of ongoing human suffering.

We have included not only stories, but theological and ethical reflections on the process and importance of storytelling – of narrative. While the importance of narrative has been a central issue in much contemporary theology and ethics, this theory is rarely demonstrated with as much power as it is in the TRC hearings. This reflection on narrative is central to a number of the contributions to the book. Denise Ackermann combines a profound reflection on the need for and place of lament in theology and public life with a poignant narrative of her own, while Russel Botman reflects on how narrative theology is being translated into daily practice by the stories being told at the hearings. These function, he argues, as keys to unlock the "metaphorical locking devices" created by apartheid.

We have also included some critical voices in the articles we have gathered. Willa Boesak reflects on the TRC in terms of an ethics of vengeance, questioning the easy talk of amnesty and forgiveness without reparation and restitution, and Robin Petersen warns of the possible consequences of white South Africans not responding to the "politics of grace" which have been shown them.

Most of the articles we have gathered, however, are critically supportive of the TRC process. We hope that the arguments that are advanced in these reflections will provide theological and ethical substance to this support.

In 1985 a group of theologians issued a powerful and controversial critique of the theological abuse of the notion of reconciliation in the now famous *Kairos Document*. One of the primary participants in the shaping of that document, Molefe Tsele, headed up the tenth-year anniversary conference to reflect upon the *kairos* process which was convened by the Institute for Contextual Theology in 1995. Tsele makes an important contribution to this study by his analysis of the TRC in light of the twin motifs of *kairos* and *Jubilee*. Tsele's article, together with three substantial theological reflections on the issues raised by the TRC, makes up the remainder of this section. These other articles include an essay on the notions of confession, guilt, truth and forgiveness in the Christian tradition by the eminent systematic theologian, Dirkie Smit. There is also an extremely important and systematic reflection on the biblical notion of reconciliation by Wolfram Kistner. There is indeed much food for reflection here. The final essay in the section, by Cornel du Toit of Unisa, returns us to the theme of dealing with the past and the centrality of memory in the process.

The concluding section brings together three essays on challenges to the Church presented by the TRC and its process. Charles Villa-Vicencio, now Director of Research for the TRC, presents a personal reflection on his involvement in the TRC and the challenge that this presents to the English-language churches, while Etienne de Villiers from the University of Pretoria develops this theme in the context of the Afrikaans-establishment churches.

The theological and ethical reflections contained in the book are framed by two contributions from outside these fields. In the first, the Minister of Justice, Dullah Omar, under whose authority the Commission functions, gives a brief introduction to the TRC. In the second, Terry Dowdall of the *Trauma Centre for Victims of Violence and Torture* provides an important contribution on the psychological aspects and challenges of the TRC. We have also included in an appendix a transcript of the Religious Service for the Commissioning of the Commissioners.

In our brief to contributors, we asked them to keep academic references to a minimum, as we wanted to make the book accessible to a broad public. We trust that we as editors have ensured that this goal has been accomplished. We hope that anyone interested in the work of the TRC in general, and in some deeper theological and ethical reflections on the process in particular, will find much sustenance in the book. The TRC process is truly proving to be a cathartic one for the nation. We believe that in rooting this emotional healing process in the soil of reflection, individuals and religious communities may respond more completely to it.

We thank those who have shared their stories with us through their reflections. We thank too Linette Viljoen at Human and Rousseau for her enthusiasm for the project and her patience with us; the various authors and institutions that have given us permission to use their work; Nicia Smith for her "scanning and typing"; and our families for their support.

This book is dedicated to all the victims of apartheid, both those whose stories we will hear, and those whose stories may never be told. May they endure as living witnesses to the trauma through which we have all come, reminding us never to forget.

INTRODUCTORY THEMES

Fr Michael Lapsley

Bearing the Pain in Our Bodies

Interview for BBC Radio, 13 April 1994

In April 1990 the apartheid regime sent me a letter bomb to my home in Zimbabwe. I survived with the loss of both hands and an eye.

Today, I am the chaplain to a Trauma Centre for Victims of Violence and Torture in Cape Town. We work with a range of people who have suffered as a result of political and organised violence. This includes people who were imprisoned, detained and tortured; people who were exiled from South Africa, people who have suffered as a result of urban and rural violence. We also work with asylum seekers and political refugees from other countries in Africa.

Common to many of our clients is the search for the healing of the memories. Together with all of South Africa's people, we are seeking to come to terms with the past. How do we free ourselves from what we have done and what has been done to us as well as what we have failed to do? Our ability to create a just and humane society today and tomorrow is profoundly related to our response to the apartheid years.

People in South Africa are beginning to come forward to tell their stories. Today I would like to tell my story. My own is intertwined with the story of the South African Nation.

I was born and brought up in New Zealand. During adolescence I read Father Trevor Huddlestone's *Naught for Your Comfort*. Fr Huddlestone shocked the world with his chilling description of apartheid, including a heart-rending account of forced removals. It made an indelible impression on me. I knew apartheid was evil and the opposite of the Christian Gospel. Little did I know that South Africa would eventually become home and change my life for ever.

I became a member of a religious order called the Society of the Sacred Mission in Australia. I was ordained to the priesthood in 1973. In the same year, I was transferred to South Africa to become a university student and subsequently a university chaplain. In my naivety, I had thought that South Africa would be composed of oppressed people and oppressors but that I would belong to a third category called the human community. The all-embracing system of apartheid, however, decreed that my colour would make me a member of the oppressor group.

As a Christian I believed that we are called to love God and our neighbour. But I was unable to fulfil God's command to love my neighbour as I loved myself. Apartheid prevented me from being a neighbour to any person of colour.

I felt that apartheid had changed me from a human being into a white man. My value and every aspect of my life was defined by my pigmentation, not because I was a child of God made in God's image and likeness. It had robbed me of my humanity.

Only if apartheid was completely destroyed would I be able to love my neighbour as myself and so fulfil the commandment of God.

I joined the struggle to liberate South Africa, not as a favour to people of colour. I needed to recover my own humanity. I needed to fulfil the command of God. I sought to act in solidarity with the majority of South Africa's people as they sought to free themselves from the yoke of apartheid.

It was less than four years after arriving in South Africa that I was expelled from the country. When I left South Africa in 1976 there were no marks on my body. At the same time, South Africa tore me apart as a human being. Was I crazy or was the society crazy? Apartheid had not damaged my body, it had severely attacked my soul. The Bible tells us not to worry about those who kill the body but rather those who kill the soul.

When I first left South Africa, I went to live in Lesotho. Le-

18

sotho is completely surrounded by South Africa. I continued my studies at the National University of Lesotho. They told me that I was the first white student to transfer from a South African university. There was one other white student. I found myself accepted and related to as an individual human being and not as a category. The raw wounds to my soul began to heal. Perhaps the Book of Genesis was right after all: "Then God said, 'Let us make humankind in our image, according to our likeness'" (Gen 1:26).

I came to the conclusion that apartheid was an option for death carried out in the name of the Gospel of life. Therefore it was an issue of faith to oppose apartheid and support the struggle for liberation. The problem was a faith problem, a theological problem. The bad faith took a political form in the denial of the vote to the majority. The solution had also to take a political form. It took sixteen years before I returned to South Africa.

From 1983 to 1992, I lived in Zimbabwe. For about three years I lived with armed police guards because the Zimbabwean authorities had information that I was on a South African Government's hit list. As my work was pastoral and theological and not military, why was I considered to be a threat? Perhaps it was my theology and my words which were a problem. I tried in my own small way to be a voice of hope within the exiled community.

Of course we were not the first people to live in exile. I was often reminded of the words of the prophet Jeremiah together with the words of the Psalmist.

Jeremiah 29:4-7

[4] This is what the LORD Almighty, the God of Israel, says to all those I carried into exile from Jerusalem to Babylon: [5] "Build houses and settle down; plant gardens and eat what they produce. [6] Marry and have sons and daughters; find wives for your sons and give your daughters in marriage, so that they too may have sons and daughters. Increase in number there; do not decrease. [7] Also, seek the peace and prosperity of the city to which I have carried you into exile. Pray to the LORD for it, because if it prospers, you too will prosper."

Psalms 137:1-6

[1] By the rivers of Babylon we sat and wept when we remembered Zion. [2] There on the poplars we hung our harps . . .[4] How can we sing the songs of the LORD while in a foreign land? [5] If I forget you, O Jerusalem, may my right hand forget [its skill] . [6] May my tongue cling to the roof of my mouth if I do not remember you, if I do not consider Jerusalem my highest joy.

Finally the day of salvation began to dawn. The pressure became too great. On February 2, 1990 the announcement came. Nelson Mandela was to be released and negotiations would begin.

We were the survivors. Soon we would return home.

The De Klerk government began to talk of apartheid as a mistake but there were no words of repentance or acknowledgement of evil.

On April 28, 1990, I opened a letter bomb hidden inside the pages of two religious magazines. It was sent from South Africa to my home in Zimbabwe.

I did not lose consciousness and I did not go into shock and the doctors did not understand why that was so.

Personally, I am grateful that I can remember and that it's not a memory that haunts me either. It is a memory that I can live with. I felt the presence of God with me in that bombing, sharing in my crucifixion. In the midst of indescribable pain, I also felt that Mary the mother of Jesus who had watched her son being crucified somehow understood what it was that I was going through.

I had no role model. I did not know a human being who had lost both hands. I had no basis of comparison to say that such a person is living his life. For a little bit of the time I thought it would have been better to have died because would life be life in any meaningful sense.

For the first three months after I was bombed, I was totally dependent on other human beings. There was nothing that I was able to do for myself.

Isaiah 52:13-15

[13] *See, my servant will* act wisely; *he will be raised and lifted up and highly exalted* [14] *Just as there were many who were*

appalled at him – his *appearance was so disfigured beyond that of any man* and his form marred *beyond human likeness* – [15] *so will he sprinkle many* nations, *and kings will* shut *their* mouths *because* of him. *For what they were not told they will see, and what* they *have not heard they* will *understand.* (Roman mine.)

Whilst I was in hospital in Harare I remembered this particular passage from Isaiah. What I also remembered was an image from Orthodoxy, that of the Saviour on the cross with one leg shorter than the other. And I remembered this particular image of the Christ figure, and of course that is an image which echoes that passage in Isaiah.

It is the opposite of western Christian imagery. Because in the Western Christian tradition, Jesus is the perfect white male figure.

I discovered that disability *is the norm of the human community.* It is not the exception. Disability and incompleteness are the norms.

In my view, to receive a letter bomb is to become a specific focus of evil in the world. People from all over the world responded with a flood of messages assuring me of their prayers and love and support. I became a focus of all that is beautiful in the human community – the ability to be kind, generous, loving and compassionate. This included people who are religious and those who are not.

I realised that if I became filled with hatred, bitterness, self-pity and desire for revenge, I would remain a victim for ever. It would consume me. It would eat me alive. God and people of faith and hope enabled me to make my bombing redemptive – to bring the life out of the death, the good out of the evil. I was enabled to grow in faith, in commitment to justice, in compassion.

Yes, I do grieve, and will always grieve especially for my hands. At times I experience great frustration. It is not easy to cope with being stared at wherever you go.

However, I am no longer a victim, nor even simply a survivor, I am a victor over evil, hatred and death.

I suppose it was by being radically, physically wounded that I discovered just how important healing is. When I was in hospital, I said to myself: For me now the struggle against apartheid is the struggle to get well, to return, to live my life as fully, as joyfully, as completely as possible. That is my victory.

Today my commitment to the struggle for liberation is played out in a commitment to the process of healing the land and healing the people.

All of us have memories of the past – memories of what we have done and what has been done to us. Happy memories and sad memories. Joyous memories and painful memories. Memories that give us strength and memories that may still be destroying us. Memories that have healed and memories that have not. Memories that we tried to bury and memories which we failed to bury. We have individual memories and collective memories. In South Africa we have very divided memories.

Within the country there was psychological and physical torture on a massive scale. The apartheid regime and all who supported it carries responsibility for the loss of millions of lives throughout the whole region of Southern Africa. Significant sections of the population were deaf and blind to what was happening and to their root causes, even when the whole world tried to tell them.

But should we not simply forgive and forget the past? Let us look first at the question of forgetting. For Christians, we need to remind ourselves that we belong to a remembering religion. "Remember when you were slaves in Egypt", is a constant refrain of the Old Testament.

The words of Jesus: "Do this in memory of me", are said at every Eucharist.

The question is not one of forgetting but rather it is the problem of how do we heal our memories? How do we stop our memories from destroying us?

Forgiveness, yes – that is always the Christian calling – but no-one should suggest that forgiveness is glib, cheap or easy. What does it mean to forgive those who have not confessed, those who have not changed their lives, those who have no interest in making it up to the relatives of victims and the survivors of their crimes? If you forgive a murderer, does that mean there should be no justice?

How do we achieve reconciliation as a nation? Can we forgive each other for what we have done?

There are many examples in the history of nations who tried

to bury rather than face the past. No nation has ever succeeded. If we try to ignore or bury the past it will haunt us and may even destroy us.

There are millions of people in South Africa who have stories to tell from the apartheid years – stories of what they did, stories of what was done, stories of what we failed to do. Every South African has a story to tell.

The issues at stake are spiritual issues, concerned with the spiritual health of the nation. If we are filled with anger, hatred, bitterness and a desire for revenge, we will never create a just and compassionate society. If we have those feelings they need to be worked through lest they continue to consume us.

Forgiveness, healing, and reconciliation will not happen in an instant. Some say that the process will be worked out over the next hundred years. But we can assist ourselves in the process if we have the will.

Through the power of God at work in our lives we can begin to make what has happened to us redemptive – to bring the good out of the evil, the life out of the death.

We cannot be healed until we acknowledge our sickness.

As we recognise our woundedness and brokenness and seek for healing, the South African nation begins to move from being the polecat of the world to become a light to the nations.

Why did I survive a bomb that was supposed to kill? Perhaps to be a small sign of South Africa's brokenness, yes, but much more important, to be a sign that love and faith and gentleness are stronger than hatred and evil and death.

Dullah Omar
Minister of Justice

Introduction to the Truth and Reconciliation Commission

Instead of revenge
there will be reconciliation

Instead of forgetfulness
there will be knowledge and acknowledgement

Instead of rejection
there will be acceptance by a compassionate state

Instead of violations of human rights
there will be the restoration
of the moral order and respect
for the rule of law

After a long process of discussion and debate, inside and outside of Parliament, the Truth and Reconciliation Commission has finally been appointed and begun its work. It is important to understand the context in which the Truth and Reconciliation Commission takes place. The Commission is based on the final clause of the Interim Constitution which reads as follows:

This Constitution provides a historic bridge between the past of a deeply divided society characterised by strife, conflict, untold suffering and injustice, and a future founded on the recognition of human rights, democracy and peaceful co-existence and development of opportunities for all South Africans, irrespective of colour, race, class, belief or sex.

The pursuit of national unity, the well-being of all South African citizens and peace require reconciliation between the people of South Africa and the reconstruction of society.

The adoption of this Constitution lays the secure foundation for the people of South Africa to transcend the divisions and strife of the past, which generated gross violations of human rights, the transgression of humanitarian principles in violent conflicts and a legacy of hatred, fear, guilt and revenge.

These can now be addressed on the basis that there is a need for understanding but not for vengeance, a need for reparation but not retaliation, a need for *ubuntu* but not for victimisation.

In order to advance such reconciliation and reconstruction, amnesty shall be granted in respect of acts, omissions and offences associated with political objectives and committed in the course of the conflicts of the past. To this end, Parliament under this Constitution shall adopt a law determining a firm cut-off date which shall be a date after 8 October 1990 and before December 1993, and providing for the mechanisms, criteria and procedures, including tribunals, if any, through which such amnesty shall be dealt with at any time after the law has been passed.

With this Constitution and these commitments we, the people of South Africa, open a new chapter in the history of our country.

I could have gone to Parliament and produced an amnesty law – but this would have been to ignore the victims of violence entirely. We recognised that we could not forgive perpetrators unless we attempt also to restore the honour and dignity of the victims and give effect to reparation.

The question of amnesty must be located in a broader context and the wounds of our people must be recognised. I do not distinguish between ANC wounds, PAC wounds and other wounds – many people are in need of healing, and we need to heal our country if we are to build a nation which will guarantee peace and stability.

A critical question which involves all of us is how do South Africans come to terms with the past? In trying to answer this important question honestly and openly, we are fortunate in having a President who is committed to genuine reconciliation in our country and to the transformation of South Africa into a nonracial, nonsexist democracy based on a recognition of universally accepted human rights.

The President believes – and many of us support him in this belief – that the truth concerning human rights violations in our country cannot be suppressed or simply forgotten. They ought to be investigated, recorded and made known. Therefore the President supports the Truth and Reconciliation Commission. The democratic government is committed to the building up of a human rights culture in our land.

There is a commitment to break from the past, to heal the wounds of the past, to forgive but not to forget and to build a future based on respect for human rights. This new reality in the human rights situation in South Africa places a great responsibility upon all of us. Human rights is not a favour or a gift handed down as a favour by government or state to loyal citizens. It is the right of each and every citizen. Part of our joint responsibility is to help to illuminate the way, to chart the road forward and provide South Africa with beacons or guidelines based on international experiences. We must guard against dangers and pitfalls! We must involve our citizens in the debate so as to ensure that human rights is not the preserve of the few but the birthright of every citizen! We must embark upon the journey from the past, through our transition and into a new future.

I wish to stress that the objective of the exercise is not to conduct a witch-hunt or to drag violators of human rights before court to face charges. However, it must be stressed that a commission is a necessary exercise to enable South Africans to come to terms with their past on a morally accepted basis and to advance the cause of reconciliation.

I invite you to join in the search for truth without which there can be no genuine reconciliation.

Terry Dowdall

Psychological Aspects of the Truth and Reconciliation Commission

At the heart of the Truth and Reconciliation Commission's work is psychological change. This is so whether we are looking at the individual traumatised survivor, the perpetrator, the onlooker in society, the local community, the country or the family of nations. Correctly, the first focus should be the emotional damage and unresolved turmoil of thought and feeling of the survivors, but the overarching goal must be profound change in the belief and value systems that permit torture, atrocities and human rights violations to flourish. In this chapter I want to look at some of the contributions that psychologists can make to Commissions of this nature, both in service and conceptualisation.

From the outset, however, I want to make plain my conviction that in the work of the Truth and Reconciliation Commission we are involved not only in tending psychological trauma or helping facilitate national reconciliation in our country, vital though both of those goals are. We are also part of the crucial movement of our times – the human rights movement against torture, organised violence, political murder, genocide and allied human rights abuses. In the 18th and 19th centuries the movement against slavery challenged the assumptions and accepted practices of thousands of years. Over a period of little more than a hundred years, enormous gains were made, to the effect that no state today could openly trade in slaves or sanction slavery without incurring pariah status and rapidly accumulating international penalties. This human rights movement of the 20th and 21st Centuries faces a similar long haul, but we have seen that each small victory and precedent counts and that the cumulative effect can create a climate in which the common perception of human rights abuses is not that they are "regrettable but understandable" but that they are intolerable and indefensible. It is this goal which should inform our work at every level.

From the psychological perspective and allied to the point above, I want to point to the centrality of cognitions – of thoughts, beliefs, values and ideologies – at every level of the cycle of repression and resistance. Our construction of our actions and experiences – the way we make sense of them – is crucial to the understanding of the infliction and effects of organised violence, of damage, healing, rehabilitation and reconciliation. It is a key element in why some people cope with fortitude in the face of horrific abuses, whilst others fall into despair and depression; why "ordinary men" can torture prisoners entrusted to their custody, or brutally assault teenagers and then go home to a pleasant supper with their own teenage children. It also helps us to make sense of how a climate is created in which human rights violations become "acceptable", and conversely begins to open up possibilities of "innoculatory" or preventive work.

The Truth and Reconciliation Commission in International Perspective

It is important to keep the South African Truth and Reconciliation Commission in focus against the evil which it is intended to counteract, the gross human rights violations committed – primarily by the State – over the past decades. At the international and national level it is important to realise that the tragedies of assassination and murder, torture and abuse that have been played out and resisted in South Africa are part of a much broader struggle across the globe. The human rights movement and the movement against torture are the first serious international movements to challenge the right of regimes to use murder and torture as instruments to enforce state policy. Violent repression is beginning to be no longer respected as the

28

private domestic concern of states, just as wife-battering and child abuse are no longer regarded as the private domestic business of the family.

The right of governments to abuse and repress their citizens remains, however, bitterly contested ground, which is why each country that emerges from under a repressive regime and then decides how to manage the reckoning with the perpetrators is watched so closely. Since the Nuremberg trials and through a long string of Commissions of Truth, Justice and Reconciliation, the international community has been experimenting and setting precedents in making gross human rights abuse a crime for which officials may be called to account when the protection of their regime falls away. This differs from the vengeful retaliation which has existed throughout history, in that it is an attempt to return the state to civil justice and deal with the perpetrators within this system, with all the checks and balances implied. It is also commonly wedded to the goal of national reconciliation which further tempers the processes decided upon politically. The work of the Commission in South Africa will therefore impact on the unfolding international consensus on the unacceptableness of violent repression and the responsibilities of politicians, officials, policemen and soldiers for violent repressive crimes.

The Conundrums of Impunity in a Truth Commission without Justice

"Impunity" represents the most problematic aspect of a Truth and Reconciliation process. At worst it constitutes – either *de jure* or *de facto* – a blanket absolution and protection for those who committed horrific crimes "in the line of duty"; and a situation where these crimes are concealed and never confirmed or condemned by the authorities of the country. It sends an unequivocal message: it's OK to torture, rape and murder people if you do it under the umbrella of any regime's policies and orders. Impunity means never having to say you're sorry, and never having to pay for your crimes. And, of course, impunity reassures the population of abusers – those still in office and those who may occupy such posts in the future – that work as a torturer/killer is still a career option. To the extent that we condone it we risk perpetuating abusive patterns.

At the same time, however, we have to deal with the problem of how to counter impunity without imperilling reconciliation by seeming to embark on a witch-hunt against political opponents. One of the most crucial points for the well-being of society that must be established through a Truth Commission is that *no ends whatsoever justify gross human rights violations.* Any political movement that argues that torture or arbitrary murder are somehow more acceptable in the service of *their* ends becomes fatally compromised, and lays the grounds for future abuse. For this reason it is important that gross human rights abuses are recorded and treated in the same way regardless of whether they were perpetrated by the former regime or by the liberation movements. Paradoxically this gives enormous moral force to the new government and armours the state against replicating the evils of the past regime. Nationally and internationally it sends the strong message that human rights violations are unacceptable and that the rule of law stands above any party political strategies. Latin American activists have argued that when human rights abuses are condoned and ignored this has a corrosive effect on belief in a democratic society and on respect for laws and prohibitions within the general society. The concessions that were necessary in South Africa to allow the elections to go ahead have made proper justice impossible in most cases; and this is one of the flaws of the Commission in this country; but in the public nature of the hearings and the moral force with which they have been vested, the Truth and Reconciliation Commission still has a very important role to play in the restoration of respect for right and wrong in South Africa.

Counteracting the Culture of Fear and Silence
Where servants of the State (or a political movement) perpetrate gross human rights violations like torture and murder, this is normally part of a strategy to extend power and control. The intention is to collapse opposition by inducing complicity through fear. Fear is built systematically by creating the image of the monolithic all-powerful state against which the individual cannot prevail – a state which through highly organised security forces acts ruthlessly and with impunity. The citizens, and particularly those with dissident inclinations, have to grow to

30

fear the state forces, and for this reason they must know of the fate of detainees and other victims. They must see the damage done, and begin to fear for their safety and the safety of their loved ones. They need to understand that even small gestures of resistance might invite brutal retaliation. Their neighbours need to be aware of their possible contamination through association with dissidents, and the threat that they themselves may be endangered. Shocking violence, therefore, has to be common knowledge.

Simultaneously, however, torture and human rights violations are meant to be known by all but spoken of by none. People have to be taught to take for granted that safety lies in silence, and that speaking out or asking questions is dangerous. In public forums, of course, the security forces normally vigorously deny systematic involvement in torture and murder, illustrating the cynical "doublethink" that must operate in their position.

This denial, of course, points to the Achilles' heels of most repressive regimes: their sense that no matter how far they rationalise, they are doing something wrong. They therefore exhibit a grotesque hankering after respectability. Few such regimes feel liberated and confident enough to come out publicly and say: "Yes! Power and the fruits of office are what matter to us and we're going to hold on to them. We intend to murder and torture all we please, because not only does it make us feel great, but it helps to scare the people into doing exactly as we tell them!" It is a strange and pervasive phenomenon that viciousness and brutality have to be packaged in the conceptual envelope of "righteousness", particularly in mediating relations with others. It is as if there is a deep-lying common 'shaming' reference point of basic moral inhibition that regulates ordinary social relations, and to violate this and keep self-esteem intact requires an elaborate rationale – a cognitive 'cover story' about how the perpetrator is actually doing right. Where this rationale is sophisticated enough and backed by the resources of the state, it is frequently absorbed at least partially by much of the population, and sometimes despite themselves, by the victims themselves.

The 'culture of silence', then, is not just the absence of speaking out against intimidation and repression. It is a complex mix of fear, avoidance and compromise that is often entangled with

31

confused ideas from the regime's propaganda. In many cases the primary message that has been absorbed is the 'process' message – that power confers the *right to* abuse. This is one of the reasons why the Truth and Reconciliation Commission is so important to the country as a whole: left alone – just walked away from – the distorted visions absorbed during the period of repression remain unchallenged, uncorrected. The general public does not necessarily rethink its assumptions about the proper use of power; the survivors are left with the ache, the burden and confusion of the past and the sense of lessened value – that somehow the crimes committed against them did not really matter and that they are expendable – and the perpetrators remain unreconstructed, perhaps 'living to fight another day'.

The TRC, then, is first of all addressed to the two crucial groups most centrally involved: the survivors and their families, and the perpetrators.

The Perpetrators: Stripping Away the Tissue of Lies

We have seen that the repressive state constructs a sanitised, often romanticised picture of itself as the good and valiant state, guardian of the 'good culture', which is protecting the citizens against the barbarians and the wicked. Central and essential to this picture is the demonisation of the 'enemy' and the discourse of defence against threat and destruction. This is the essential rationale for the perpetrators – it is the shield for their self-esteem as they commit atrocities and violate norms that all but the most degenerate people hold.

For the perpetrators within the system, the doublethink and the manufactured rationalisations cannot be left intact. They must be unravelled and laid bare, and the Truth and Reconciliation Commission is there to put paid to the lies that the perpetrators were acting in a necessary way in a good cause. From this perspective, a key function of the Commission is to expose the individual perpetrator to the real horror and shame of his actions. It is also hopefully an inoculation against the class of potential torturers and organised killers waiting in the wings.

Do mental health workers have responsibilities towards perpetrators? Do we treat perpetrators? This is a vexed question because of the particular and personal nature of the therapeutic relationship between mental health worker and client. Strong feelings of revulsion or anger – any strong negative feelings – do not bode well for the relationship of acceptance, unconditional positive regard, and trust, that seems to be important for a good working therapeutic relationship. Countertransference has long been seen as a problem in this area in the Latin American countries, where therapists have had to confront the question: "But, would you treat a torturer ...?" Such is the feeling amongst many Latin American therapists, that the answer is: "No! – not until he has served his due punishment." In fact, some go further, insisting that the greater good of the wider society overrides even the confidentiality of the therapeutic relationship, and that if it arises in therapy that a client has been a torturer, he should be unmasked, reported by his therapist. In South Africa, some of these issues will have to be confronted by individual therapists. Many therapists would be reluctant to assist a former murderer or torturer to become more comfortable with his past actions if they plagued him now. Most would probably want to see some kind of repentance and reparation as part of the work with a perpetrator.

But, of course, at the same time we need to know and understand all we can about the processes that lead people to this position, and we cannot simply turn our backs on the problem. This area remains inadequately thought through by mental health professionals in this country.

The Survivors: Countering the Cruelty
The past fifteen years have seen an exponential increase in work and thinking about trauma survivors. The concept of Post-Traumatic Stress Disorder (PTSD) has been developed and elaborated, and a range of treatment strategies has been explored, with partial success. Particularly in the areas of politically motivated violence, torture and repression, the movement against torture has vested an enormous amount of energy in working on the development of therapies, and the number of centres treating torture survivors has grown from a handful to literally hundreds. Third-world centres – particularly those groups working within the country under repression – have vigorously challenged the narrow psychiatric diagnosis category of PTSD for torture survivors, and have pointed to the inextricable links between torture and the political context of

33

the abuse. To strip the experience of its meaning is counter-therapeutic in every way.

The survivors of repressive violence in any country, including South Africa, vary widely in the difficulties which they suffer in the aftermath of gross human rights violations. Many survivors have been able to transcend horrific abuses with varying degrees of resilience and success.

This is particularly so for those with a strong and coherent set of beliefs, either religious or political, that sustain an overarching sense of purpose and allow them to put their experiences in that perspective. For many survivors, however, the experience of torture or other abuse can be a blight which descends upon the rest of their lives. They can remain racked by intrusive memories which do not lose their painful emotional charge, and their relationship to the present is attenuated by diminished concentration and memory and emotional swings. Their illusion of invulnerability punctured, their sense of trust in their fellows severely eroded, their ability to relate intimately impaired, and their sense of self-esteem often crippled by past humiliations and perceived self-betrayals, they are often increasingly withdrawn and excluded from active social, emotional and political life.

Silence becomes a tempting option. The wish to expose and talk through the wrong that was done is often counteracted by the wish to ignore and avoid the intensely painful memories of this period. Survivors may be abetted by people close to them who equally wish to put the horrible experiences behind them. The result is often that survivors may feel misunderstood, ignored, their sacrifices unacknowledged, their pain unrecognised. They continue to collaborate in complicity with silence, as the perpetrators had intended.

In countering this situation the Truth and Reconciliation Commission is important, and can contribute to rehabilitation by breaking through the culture of silence. We all know that concealing, suppressing or repressing painful memories commonly brings in its wake psychological symptoms: stress, anxiety and depression. We also know that speaking about upsetting things in a supportive and affirming setting makes people feel better.

But many questions remain about the psychological effects of such truth commissions on survivors. Our discussions with survivors suggest that for many people who have been tortured, or have had loved ones murdered or maimed, the Truth Commission may feel like a double-edged sword. It will inevitably inflame old hurts, bring them back, and disturb the equilibrium that these people have been able to achieve. It may open old wounds at least as much as it may heal. One of the issues that has arisen frequently in discussions with torture survivors is the wish for justice and, in fact, retribution. Many people are going to feel intense anger, feelings of impotent desire for revenge, feelings of hurt and bitterness. These may well be compounded as they see the form of impunity enjoyed by the perpetrators, who will go unpunished by the law.

However, we have also seen a remarkable capacity in a great many people to overcome, to forgive, to go forward. For the TRC to succeed it will be necessary that a very clear conception of what it is about, what its possibilities and limitations are, is propagated widely and repeatedly stressed and clarified. We have seen the power of a coherent vision to sustain people in difficult times. Survivors will need a clear understanding of both the limitations of the Commission and its positive values (most of which will transcend the individual level) if they are going to make something positive of it despite its disappointments.

The potential positive benefits of the Commission in fact greatly outweigh the inherent limitations. Putting the record straight – publicly, officially, and through respected Commissioners who are clearly not just acting out a party political agenda – is of the greatest importance, since it helps develop a clear and positive sense in survivors. Albie Sachs, in an address to a psychoanalytic symposium, put it very clearly: "We need to feel that basically we did right, that we did not deserve what was inflicted upon us. This gives a sense of rightness to the world, not just to us, but to the future."

Mental health workers obviously have many roles that can be played in support of the Commission. They need to help propagate the process and rationale of the Truth Commission, to defuse unrealistic expectations and help survivors to make use of the process in a helpful way. They need to provide support groups for those who are going to give testimony and those who have given testimony, or to make available counselling where it is needed around the testimony process. Where it can be helpful, they should be supportive to natural helping networks – religious or others – that will in any event do most of the support. And, of course, they need to be available in a supportive capacity to the Truth Commissioners and others who will be in daily contact with corrosive and traumatic stories of cruelty, and are likely to suffer a creeping vicarious traumatisation in the process.

The Nation: Catharsis and Inoculation

Much has been written about the cathartic effect upon the nation of telling the truth about the abuses of the past. To some extent this is, of course, a convenient metaphor, but it remains crucial that it is clearly stated that these things happened and that they are evil. Without that point being made again and again we will be vulnerable to the perception that it is somehow acceptable for governments in power to abuse citizens and abrogate the rule of law. It has become a cliché to reiterate that those who forget the past are condemned to repeat it, but it is nonetheless true for all that. How do we see that the new generation will not forget the past? Surely there is a powerful case for incorporating a serious human rights syllabus within the school system. The school system is the most extensive entry point for change, and should be used systematically for this purpose. We need to build a vibrant multiculturalism – the 'rainbow nation' of which Tutu speaks – where tolerance of diversity is an active value. We need to instil in pupils a clear sense of human rights – and take them through repeated case studies of countries where intolerance, prejudice and hatred have been fostered, together with the consequences. They need to be taught to detect and recognise hate-speech and prejudice for what it is, and to see how unscrupulous politicians manipulate the public to achieve personal ends. Case studies, role plays and active discussion need to be fostered in these fields in the young, so that there is some active inoculation and we give teeth to the belief that "It must never happen again!"

H Russel Botman

Narrative Challenges in a Situation of Transition

Words and Stories to Deal with the Past

South Africa has taken to words and stories to deal with its past. Perhaps, more than that, to seek its future from the burning ashes of the torture, maiming and killing of the apartheid era.

Stories or narratives have become increasingly important in theology during the past decade. In most countries it has remained an intellectual debate. In South Africa we see people coming to live in and through their stories. We see people rebuilding their family names word by word as they narrate their painful histories. We are confronted by people returning from the dead in the stories that have been nurtured in the hearts of many people, victims and perpetrators. To one, a story of love; to the other, a story of hatred.

It has become vividly clear that the self-perception and world views of people are expressed in story form. They communicate, confess, forgive, and reconcile in the form of stories. Victims and perpetrators and those who thought that they were just innocent bystanders, now realise their complicity, and have an opportunity to participate in each other's humanity in story form. Each person and each community has its own history of life which is embedded in a framework of stories or narratives, which in turn is nourished by wider stories from the social and cultural context and also by the grand stories of confession, forgiveness, reconciliation and truth.

Unlocking Metaphorical Locking Devices

Many people, especially those from behind the iron curtain of apartheid, the Broederbond, Afrikaner culture, the schools of Christian-National education, and the churches of "sovereignty in their own circles", are now called out from behind the curtains. They hear stories which infringe on their own well-known stories. Their horizons have consequently been broadened.

They have grown up in places where these stories were too sensitive for their ears. They have learnt to know the difference between "sensitive" and "nonsensitive" issues. In calling issues of justice "emotional", "sensitive" and "delicate" these words became the "metaphorical locking devices" of apartheid theology and supporters of apartheid. I call them "metaphorical locking devices" because they were used to close the debate rather than to open concrete issues to public discussion. Once an issue was pronounced "sensitive and emotional" we all knew it actually meant: "let's not talk about it any further or allow any further discussion on the matter".

Those who fought against contextual theology by using these "metaphorical locking systems" were very serious about it. They used these "metaphorical locking devices" also in their local faith communities, in their local churches. Nobody was allowed to address the issues which lay behind the metaphorical locking devices. Pastors or ministers were effectively silenced, issues of justice in their own churches were effectively made invisible, and the decision-making bodies of their churches were made prophetically blind, deaf and mute. This was very dangerous because theology is born in the local community, it is nurtured there and, unfortunately, it is sometimes also "locked up" there. Metaphorical locking devices not only close the doors on justice, they also build new doors to private theologies that empower the individual and destroy the community. Members of churches where these devices were dominant often find it difficult, if not impossible, to relate to others and the otherness in people. A "metaphorical locking device", especially when it is used in the survival of a race, class or gender, not only locks others out, it also locks oneself or one's own group in.

People went further than their local churches. They took the "metaphorical locking devices" home and applied it to their own children and spouses. Subsequently, their own children became

38

blind, deaf and mute to the issues of contextuality, justice and liberation. In fact they lost sight of the truth in their own country.

The Truth and Reconciliation Commission is the most fundamental challenge to the power of these "metaphorical locking devices". The Commission challenges everybody to come to terms with a storytelling community, where the old "metaphorical locking devices" are being unlocked by the stories that come to them from behind these devices.

This Commission of seventeen men and women will, for eighteen months, be going from city to city, town to town and village to village to allow victims of apartheid to tell their stories. There is no place to hide anymore. Truth has captured the attention in the street, at the working place, in the local faith communities and the homes of many people. Every day on public television, victims are speaking. When they open their mouths the codes of the "metaphorical locking devices" are broken. Tears well up in people's eyes as they drive on the streets of our country listening to reports of these stories on their radio.

Children from local churches and homes where these "metaphorical locking devices" were applied are exposed to the national process of storytelling. And this time it is the stories of the victims that they hear. Every time they hear the stories, the contemporary miracle happens: the deaf begin to hear! And every time the mothers of the victims cry and Desmond Tutu wipes a tear, the contemporary miracle happens: the blind begin to see! And every night when they go home they know the code of the "metaphorical locking device", and the contemporary miracle happens: their mute parents begin to speak! More of their pastors, still afraid, send private, anonymous letters to the Commission to say: We are sorry! A contemporary miracle has happened, the tongue of the local apartheid churches has been touched and its silence is slowly breaking as more and more people learn the codes to the metaphorical locking devices!

Background to This Development

Unknown to many, modest discussions in a class of Prof Jaap Durand, ex-vice Rector of the University of the Western Cape, played a formative role in the embryonic phase of the debate on reconciliation and apartheid in South Africa. Jaap Durand was then professor of Systematic Theology and taught a class of which I was a member. On a certain day in 1978 a discussion ensued where we asked what the theological crux of the sin of apartheid was. We had spent many hours before then debating the ethical injustices of apartheid and now wanted to trace all of that knowledge to its theological centre. From this debate emerged the proposal "that apartheid was inherently against the gospel" and the reason for this was found in its "point of departure". "Apartheid," we said, "departs from the irreconcilability of people". Needless to say Jaap Durand played a formative role in constructing the text in our thoughts.

The question arose as to what should be done about this idea. Durand then approached Reverends Jan Mettler and Isak Mentor, two formidable leaders of the Dutch Reformed Mission Church at the time. They proposed this basic judgement on Apartheid to the Synod of the Dutch Reformed Mission Church in 1978. As can be seen from the minutes of Synod, the proposal was adopted at this historic Synod of 1978. This was the first time, as far as I know, since its mention in the Cottesloe Statement (1960), *Message to the People*, that reconciliation was officially raised in relation to debates on apartheid.

Allan Boesak, then member of the executive of the Dutch Reformed Mission Church, confronted the World Alliance of Reformed Churches General Council of 1982 in Ottowa with the logical conclusion to be drawn from the decision of the 1978 synod of his church. The conclusion was accepted that if apartheid was essentially anti-evangelical (meaning, against the heart of the gospel), then any theological defence of apartheid amounts to heresy.

Although the heresy theme captured most of the attention within the debate among Dutch Reformed Churches, "reconciliation" became a flagship, a "liberating metaphorical device". The pregnant meaning of the word itself aroused hope, gave birth to prayers for the end to apartheid in the interest of a reconciled future.

A Liberating Metaphorical Device?
Unrelated to the process in the circles of the Dutch Reformed Churches, a national Kairos event took the issue of reconciliation, or should I say "irreconcilability", further. This strand in

South African theology that was developed in the Kairos Document is the brand of Contextual Theology that arose from the flames of the townships in 1985. These "flames of the township" brought Contextual theologians from all persuasions together in pursuit of the theological challenge of the moment. The question was how the church was challenged by the flames of the township. The Kairos Document, signed by 153 Christians, united the broad forces of Contextual Theology in South Africa. The Kairos Document maintained that the conflict in South Africa is between an oppressor and the oppressed. These two represent *irreconcilable causes or interests*, according to the document.

In the 1990s the situation was dramatically altered by the unbanning of the ANC and its allies. Joe Slovo, then Secretary General of the Communist Party in South Africa, proposed the adoption of the "sunset-clause" (1992). The "sunset-clause" in effect challenged the strict, exclusive understanding of reconciliation in Kairos theology. The African National Congress and the South African Communist Party subsequently adopted the "sunset-clause" as a policy position. The "sunset-clause" is a pragmatic acceptance that the revolution against the Pretoria Regime could not be taken to its conclusion. The "enemy" was overcome politically, but was not destroyed militarily. Negotiations with a greater willingness to compromise were eventually accepted as the correct response in view of these sociopolitical conditions. First the "talks about talks", then the Kempton Park negotiations ensued, and in the same spirit, the nation of South Africa thereafter elected its first democratic government on 27 April 1994, and finally negotiated the contents of the Constitution of the new South Africa.

Dullah Omar, Minister of Justice, initiated the process that finally led to the establishment of the Truth and Reconciliation Commission. However, not everybody accepted the idea of "reconciliation" as a "liberating metaphorical device". In fact, a certain division can be seen among Kairos theologians. The contribution of Molefe Tsele, elsewhere in this book, bears testimony to the "frustration" experienced in some circles of the Kairos theologians.

Not everybody agrees that reconciliation is a "liberating metaphorical device".

41

We Have Been Criticised

Some criticisms were levelled against the statements on reconcilability in the Kairos Document. The messianic language used to justify the proposal for a prophetic theology of direct action was also criticised. José Miguez Bonino, the Argentinean Professor of Theology at the University of Buenos Aires, questioned the wisdom of the Kairos theologians in addressing the struggle in eschatological language: The God of the enemy is not only an idol, it is Satan, the anti-Christ. He made the following crucial statement:

> Those of us who have confronted repressive and reactionary regimes who have used this theological discourse to justify the violation of all human laws and values (and this is not far from the experience of our sisters and brothers in South Africa) know what it can mean to a nation. The Church has also a long experience in this demonizing of historical struggles (Miguez Bonino 1985: 56).

Clifford Green criticised what he called the weak christological centre of the Kairos Document. He points to the position of the Barmen Declaration of the German Christians who opposed Hitler. Christology was used to combat idolatry. The highest obedience belongs to Christ. He pointed out that a stronger christological emphasis would have clarified the point that God is not revealed anywhere else but in Jesus Christ. This would have given new strength to the document's arguments on the issues of power and reconciliation. Green addresses with great concern the problem of the doctrine of reconciliation of the Kairos Document. He expresses appreciation for the way in which the document describes the dynamics of repentance and new life, which are the two sides of the Christian doctrine of reconciliation. However, since it lacks the christological concentrations he found the statements on reconciliation in the document less than adequate. Green adamantly maintains that what is "biblical" should be more sharply focused on what is "Christological" (Green 1986: 49-55).

The Sunset-Clause and the Rising Sun of Reconciliation

We can embrace "reconciliation" as a "liberating metaphorical device". Bonhoeffer's sermon on *Thy Kingdom Come* reminds people that are in situations of transformation and reorientation about a strange story from the Old Testament. Jacob fled from his home and lived for many years in a foreign country in a state of enmity with his brother. Then the urge to return home and to his brother became insistent. He discovered later that it was only a small river that separated him from his brother. As he prepared to cross the river, he was stopped. A stranger wrestled with him. From this struggle a blessing was born: the sunrise!

Then the sun rises on Jacob, and he proceeds into the promised land, limping because his thigh has been put out of joint. The way is clear, the dark door to the land of promise has been broken open. The blessing has come from out of the curse, and now the sun shines upon him.

That the way of all of us into the land of promise leads through the night, that we also enter it as those who are perhaps curiously scarred from the struggle with God, the struggle for his kingdom and his grace, and that we enter the land of God and of our brother (and sister) as limping warriors – all these things we Christians have in common with Jacob. And we know that the sun is destined also for us, and this knowledge allows us to bear with patience the time of wandering and waiting and believing that is imposed upon us. But beyond Jacob, we know something else. We know it is not we who must go; we know that He comes to us ... That is why we pray, "Thy kingdom come to us".

BIBLIOGRAPHY

Bonhoeffer, D. 1979. "*Thy Kingdom Come*: The prayer of the church for God's Kingdom on Earth" published in Godsey J. D. 1979. *Preface to Bonhoeffer: The Man and Two of His Shorter Writings*. Fortress: Philadelphia. Translated from the original German version *Dein Reich komme* edited by Eberhard Bethge in 1957.

Bonino, J. M. 1985. "Challenge to the Church: A Comment on the Kairos Document" in PCR Information, *Challenge to the Church: A Theological Comment in the Political Crisis in South Africa, The Kairos Document and Commentaries*, World

Council of Churches, Programme to Combat Racism.
Geneva: WCC
Green, C. 1986. *Christology and Tyranny* (Kairos Document).
JTSA, Nr 55: 49-55

THEOLOGICAL AND
ETHICAL REFLECTION

Denise Ackermann

On Hearing and Lamenting: Faith and Truth-Telling

*The expectation that one can glide through
history unpunished and rewrite one's
own biography [is one of] the traditional
Central European delusions. Whoever
fears to look his own past in the face
must necessarily fear what is to come.
Lies cannot save us from lies.*

Vaclav Havel

I cannot recall his name. But I can still see his troubled face. It was a couple of years ago in my living room. He was a member of a group of Afrikaans theology students from Stellenbosch University. We had spent the afternoon talking about Christian spirituality. A few members of the group stayed on to continue the discussion over a glass of wine. In a strangled voice, he said: "My parents lied to me, my school lied to me, our leaders lied to me, the church lied to me. I don't even know about God anymore. I have put him outside my house. I don't know anything anymore."

This young man's anguish vividly illustrates the dilemma of many young white people born and raised in the apartheid era. Lies, dissimulations, misconceptions, ignorance, apathy, heads buried in tons of sand, were the diet of the past. And now the truth is being spoken. Through the work of the Truth and Reconciliation Commission, many white South Africans are being confronted head on with the truth about the apartheid years. The murders of those resisting apartheid, the massacres of communities of people, our involvement in the dirty wars in neighbouring states, fear and terror tactics against ordinary people, the list of crimes against humanity is seemingly endless. Is it possible that truth was not heard before? What can whites do who are filled with shame and guilt on hearing the truth?

Historians, political scientists, sociologists and psychologists deal with these questions from their particular disciplines and contexts. I am a white woman who is a Christian theologian. My attempts to reflect on the dilemma of this young man, whom I shall call Johan, flow from my accountability as a white South African, my interest in Christian spirituality, my perspective as a woman and my concern for the immeasurable wounds inflicted by apartheid on both blacks and whites. I am disturbed by the inclination in my own community to want to rub out the past in an unseemly haste to be part of the present. Recently, in a thoughtful work on politics and forgiveness entitled *An Ethic for Enemies,* Donald Shriver recounts an interview between a reporter and Professor Kiyoko Takeda Cho, professor of history at the International Christian University in Tokyo. "In general Japanese tend to forget the past, thinking that it can be washed away," she said. "But I always tell my students that recognizing what we have done in the past is a recognition of ourselves. By conducting a dialogue with our past, we are searching how to go forward" (1995: 138). The desire to go forward but to do so in a manner which is truly healing and reconciling, prompts the writing of this piece.

Accountability and Awareness

Can there be *accountability* without understanding and without knowledge? To those who plead ignorance, who say "But I did not know", the answer, in the words of Adrienne Rich, is: "[We] are born both innocent and accountable" (1986: 148).

We are innocent in the sense that we do not choose the place, time and condition into which we are born. We all carry within ourselves the behaviour patterns and assumptions of the group we belong to. At the same time all of us are in the process of making history. We have a choice to become consciously historical. We can, according to Rich in *Blood, Bread and Poetry*, become "a person who tries for memory and con-nectedness against amnesia and nostalgia, who tries to describe her or his journeys as accurately as possible – or to become a technician of amnesia and nostalgia, one who dulls the imagination by starving it or feeding it with junk food" (p 145). I agree with Rich that life consists of constantly making choices. We choose "to know or not to know, to fight if necessary for the past that has been withheld from us or to remain ignorant, hoping perhaps that 'if I don't know, I won't have to move'" (p 153).

We do not know because we choose not to know. Dorothee Sölle in her moving work *Suffering*, quotes Rabbi Bunam: The sins which man commits – these are not his greatest crime … The great crime of man is that he can turn at every moment, and does not do so (p 3). By choosing not to know, by knowing a little and saying "What's the use of protesting anyway?" and, in Sölles words by "screaming too softly", we deliberately choose powerlessness and apathy. The dominant whites and those who supported them in the old regime, were hardly without power, specifically power over people. Yet they lacked moral and spiritual power, that reciprocal and collaborative energy which engages us personally and communally with God and with one another in such a way that power becomes synonymous with the vitality of living fully and freely. According to Sölle, embracing apathy (which in Greek literally means "non-suffering"), means opting "for a social condition in which people are so dominated by the goal of avoiding suffering that it becomes a goal to avoid human relationships and contacts altogether" (p 36). Apartheid was the perfect system for creating apathy by its many mechanisms which prevented contact among people. Yes, we can be both innocent and accountable.

As a woman doing theology, I find the idea of relationship to be the very opposite of powerlessness and apathy. Being in relation is central to my understanding of myself, my community, my world and my God. We live in a web of relationships and we are, by our very nature, beings who find ourselves in relationship with others. Relationships involve give-and-take. Being in a loving relationship with myself enables me to love you as your love for me enables me to love myself more. My love for God, although it can never approach God's love for me, is still in essence a two-way affair. Once we understand that our lives are made up of many and diverse relationships which are mutual, we cannot help but become accountable to one another. We are accountable for whatever we do which breaks, damages, or, on the other hand, which nurtures or restores relationships. Accountability in relationships necessitates an acute awareness of injustice and a resolve to love in such way that advances the common good of all. This is what the Reign of God is about. Jesus' announcement that "The Kingdom of God is at hand" (Matt 10:7) holds before us a vision of justice, love, freedom, equality, peace and wholeness in which all our relationships are joyful, just, and loving.

Accountability is, however, not limited to being faithful only to the values and vision of the community from which one comes. Johan's parents, his school and his church doubtless saw themselves accountable to their particular vision for South Africa. But accountability is ultimately tested in the reality of the well-being of all. I am accountable for your welfare, and yours and yours, in the sense that I may not act in any way which places it in jeopardy.

The work of the Truth and Reconciliation Commission is an exercise in accountability. It seeks to restore a culture of accountability by allowing the truth to be spoken and responsibility to be taken for wrongdoing in the past. I believe that it also stands for something more universal than its particular prescribed tasks for the next few years. It offers all South Africans the opportunity to reflect on our individual and communal accountability for actions which have fractured relationships, which have been unjust, oppressive and discriminating.

As I write these words, I know, with a deep sadness as a woman, that truth and reconciliation can only truly take place when we have the courage and insight to face *all* manifestations of lack of accountability. Once the particular vulnerability and suffering of poor women, children and old people under oppressive, discriminating political and social practices is heard and understood, we shall be on the path to true reconciliation.

Accountability requires *awareness*. The well-known Jesuit spiritual guide Anthony de Mello describes the spiritual quality of awareness as "waking up". In other words, it is the opposite of apathy, the opposite of being uncaring and uninvolved with one's neighbour, being out of relationship. Johan, like many white South Africans, grew up in an atmosphere which lacked spiritual awareness, a further terrible indictment of the system of apartheid. Of course most of us, whether we are a party to race, class or gender discrimination, do not want to wake up. We do not want to be happy unconditionally, we do not want to love unconditionally, we do not therefore want to be in unconditional relationship with others. We are ready to be happy and to love provided we have this or that or the other, or provided the other is like this or like that. We believe that our happiness and our well-being are based on conditions. Then the day comes when the house begins to crumble. Harsh realities can contribute to our waking up. The old order changes and for Johan this meant deep confusion. Johan "heard" a new reality.

Now truth is being spoken. There are no guarantees that it will be heard by every one. Hearing truth does not lie in merely hearing words. Truth is sighted suddenly when an attitude of willingness to discover something new is born. To "hear" truth we have to be able to unlearn almost everything we think we "know". We begin to wake up, we become aware. Openness to the truth, no matter where it is going to lead one, is *faith*. De Mello emphasises that faith is not belief. "Your beliefs give you a lot of security, but faith is insecurity. You don't know. You're ready to follow and you're open, you're wide open! You're ready to listen" (1990: 18). In order to be a fully awake human being one must have the readiness to learn something new. Perceptively De Mello points out that "The chances that you will wake up are in direct proportion to the amount of truth you can take without running away". He continues: "... nobody is afraid of the unknown. What you really fear is the loss of the known."

The entire apartheid edifice rested on the fear of whites that they would lose the known. It was a condition of ut-most spiritual apathy and lack of awareness. Patriarchy as a pervasive social system of male dominance also rests on fear of loss and also results in uncaring and unaware attitudes. Awareness about the pervasive evil of race oppression is essential to the healing of our country. So is the recognition of and repentance for the evil of gender oppression. Waking up to the "truth" cannot be restricted to a single self-selected arena of our lives.

51

We are accountable for our lack of awareness. Equally, we are capable of waking up. Being awake means that we will hear the truth, accept accountability and dedicate ourselves to reconciliation.

Lament as a Public Action for Reconciliation

Adrienne Rich writes that "Breaking silences, telling our tales, is not enough. We can value that process – and the courage it may require – without believing that it is an end in itself. Historical responsibility has, after all, to do with action – where we place the weight of our existences on the line, cast our lot with others, move from an individual consciousness to a collective one" (p 145). She cautions that we all need to begin with individual consciousness. Individual consciousness begins with awareness of suffering. It begins with waking up. Having come alive, we now need to act.

Johan's story speaks of a painful awakening. Through the work of the Truth and Reconciliation Commission, the consciousness of many other young Afrikaners is now being flooded with stories of suffering, of torture, of alienation and of grief. Profound questions about what it means to have faith, about human suffering, shame and guilt, about the nature of God, surface in a time of awakening. "What can I do now?" many may wonder. Is reconciliation possible?

I am concerned that whites in this country should not miss out a crucial step in the process to reconciliation. This concern prompts me to suggest that we need to *lament* the injustice and the pain of the past before we can hope for meaningful reconciliation. For some it may seem wholly inappropriate to suggest lament at a time when there is much to celebrate. But if we do not deal with past injustice and suffering both by hearing it and lamenting, it will continue to haunt our spirits and sully our efforts to heal our society. Others will point out that lament is the prerogative of the suffering victims. After all, what have whites to lament? Yes, it is true that lament in the scriptures expresses the cry of the suffering. But I suggest that repentant whites need to cry out to God for deliverance from our murky past and for healing from the wounds that oppressors inflict on themselves. Thus, the particular suffering born out of the awareness of our role in the history of our country should also be lamented.

Public lamenting of this kind is not unknown in our history. For forty years a small group of white women found a unique way of expressing grief and anger over injustice and the need for change. I am referring to the Black Sash, a women's organisation for human rights which, throughout its history, doggedly opposed Afrikaner nationalism and its apartheid vision. This the women of the Black Sash did in a number of ways: by protesting, informing, lobbying and by their indefatigable work in advice offices at various centres in South Africa. Their most visible and often most reviled public activity was to stand silently in public places with black sashes across their chests, overtly lamenting injustice. These public "stands" became a familiar part of protest politics in South Africa and once they were forbidden in terms of the Riotous Assemblies Act, the women continued to stand – not in a group, but ten metres apart! The courageous acts of these women as members of a secular body, prompt me as a Christian to ask what has happened to lament as a public act in the practice of our faith?

It appears that Western Christianity has lost its ability to lament and acts of lamentation have disappeared from our prayers and our worship. Yet, according to Claus Westermann in his work *Praise and Lament in the Psalms* (1981: 259-280), lamenting was a natural part of life as depicted in both the Hebrew and the Christian scriptures. In the theology of the Hebrew scriptures, lamenting was usually related to events concerning the deliverance of the people of Israel, although individual accounts of lamenting are also recorded. The act of lamenting formed a sequence as seen in Deut 26:5-11 and Exod 1-15: first a cry of distress, followed by a hearkening (promise of deliverance) and then a response by those that have been saved (such as praise of God). Various Psalms, such as 22, 73, 88 and 119 also attest to this sequence. Lament issues from the cry of the individual, "Out of the depths I cry to thee, O Lord!" (Ps 130), or the people "Then we cried to the Lord" (Deut 26:7) seeking God's face in moments of need. Individual laments appear early in the stories of the patriarchs and their families. We find Rebecca lamenting (Gen 25:22, 27:46), and we hear the cry of Hagar for her child (Gen 21:16). Later in the time of the kings there is the lament of the childless Hannah (1 Sam 1) and unique in the Bible, the theme of lament throughout the book of Job. National lament is tied to God's activity as saviour. Salvation, says

Westermann (260) is experienced as the hearing of the call of distress (Exod 3:7). The Hebrews were not afraid to ask how God could allow them, the chosen people, to suffer so much. In essence, lament is the language of suffering and its function is to appeal to God's compassion. As Westermann remarks, there is not a single line in the Hebrew scriptures which "would forbid lamentation or which would express the idea that lamentation had not a place in a healthy and good relationship with God" (264).

In the Gospels and indeed in the rest of the New Testament there is no suggestion that faith in Jesus Christ would prevent Christians from lamenting. Westermann continues: "Certainly in the Gospels the actions of Jesus of Nazareth are characterized by the compassion he evidenced for those who implored him to help them in their need... In the passion story the lament of the ancient people of God (Ps 22) is placed on the lips of Jesus" (p 264-265). Why then is the idea of lamenting so foreign to modern Christians? Is it evidence of how Greek thought, in particular the ethic of Stoicism, has crept into Western Christianity which advocates the bearing of suffering without complaining or lamenting?

Sölle, whose work *Suffering* delves into the nature of suffering, identifies three phases necessary for understanding and overcoming suffering (70-74). These phases are applicable in the South African context to those who have been the victims of suffering, to those who have remained silent, to those who have tolerated injustice and are now confronted with the truth, and to those who mourn the evils of the past and seek change. The first phase is one of muteness and lack of comprehension. Once "awareness" has dawned, we can move to the second phase, a language of lament, of crying, of pain, a language that at least says what the situation is (70). But lamenting is not an end in itself. No psalm ends with lamentation. It is always followed by a petition. According to Sölle, the second phase is "an indispensable step on the way to the third stage, in which liberation and help for the unfortunate can be organized. The way leads out of isolated suffering through communication (by lament) to the solidarity in which change occurs" (74). Thus lamenting presses beyond itself towards change. Change produces conflict, as the women of the Black Sash know only too well. Lamenting whites will face resistance, for the very act of lament calls for accountability and for awareness, not something everyone is ready for.

This is a time to move from muteness to lament. Lamenting offers Johan and many others like him a language in which to communicate pain, grief and disillusionment and to seek God's compassionate presence in the work of healing. It is a language which should be spoken publicly and how better can we do this than by retrieving lament in the ritual actions of communities of faith? Here, within the body of believing people, space and time can be made in liturgies for the engagement of the entire community in acts of lamentation, followed by acts of reconciliation.

The goal of public lament is healing. Healing is a very ancient aspect of religion and traditionally women have been primary healers in society. The Black Sash, as a group of women, earned themselves the tribute from Nelson Mandela of having been "the conscience of the white nation" by their public mourning and their dogged work for justice and their efforts in dealing with the wounds of the apartheid system. Women of faith can take a leaf from their book. We can, in our religious institutions, raise our voices in lament and seek the reconciliation we all need so sorely. Experience, however, has taught us that male dominance of church structures and liturgies is not friendly to change initiated by women. But, undaunted by the patriarchs, we must speak out, for this is a grave matter which challenges the very core of the Christian faith. No reconciliation is possible without repentance. The call to lament is an appeal to all, both to the victims and to the repentant perpetrators of suffering, to engage in public acts of mourning which will enable true reconciliation and healing to take place.

To lament psychologically, culturally, socially and as people of faith because of shame, guilt, disillusionment and disenchantment, is at the core of the contemporary struggle to find meaning and identity as whites in contemporary South Africa. Lamenting will enable us to break with the past, not to forget it. It will release us into the space of transition between our past and hope for a reconciled future. In his remarkable speech to the Bundestag on May 8, 1985, the president of the Federal Republic of Germany, Richard Freiherr von Weizsäcker cautioned Germans that those who closed their eyes to the past become blind to the present. "Whoever does not wish to remember inhumanity becomes susceptible to the dangers of new infection" (Shriver 110). Young white South Africans like young Germans have been bequeathed a heavy legacy and "all of us, whether guilty or not, whether old or young, must accept the past" (110). This we do in order to be able to embrace the future.

Spurred by Dom Helder Camara's cry in Sölle's work: "How much longer will anti-communism have to serve as a pretext for the support of injustices that cry to heaven? How much longer, under the pretext of fighting the terrorists, will there be a use of terrorism by the police and military authorities?" (34). I want to conclude by recounting the story of another young man, called Bernie. After school Bernie was called up into the army. After his basic training he was sent to "the border". Soon "the border" was crossed and he found himself in action in Angola. What he saw and what he had to do, I do not know. But I do know that those months changed his life forever. On his return he suffered nightmares, much insomnia and prolonged periods of depression. He sought to blunt his pain in all the ways we humans know of. He married and got divorced twice. Fifteen months after his last attempt at marriage, he killed himself. Bernie is one of many young white men who were lied to by their leaders, a tool in an evil system. I lament the deception thrust on him and many others. I lament their suffering and the suffering of their victims. I mourn for Bernie. He was my son-in-law.

WORKS CONSULTED
De Mello, Anthony 1990. *Awareness*. London: HarperCollins
Rich, Adrienne 1986. *Blood, Bread, and Poetry. Selected Prose 1979-1985*. New York: W. W. Norton
Ruether, Rosemary Radford 1985. *Women-Church. Theology and Practice of Feminist Liturgical Communities*. San Francisco: Harper and Row
Shriver, Donald W Jr 1995. *An Ethic for Enemies: Forgiveness in Politics* New York: Oxford University Press
Sölle, Dorothee 1975. *Suffering,* tr. E. R. Kalin. Philadelphia: Fortress Press
Westermann, Claus 1981. *Praise and Lament in the Psalms*, tr. K.R. Crim and R.N. Soulen. Edinburgh: T. T. Clark

Robin Petersen

The Politics of Grace and the Truth and Reconciliation Commission

In articulating the relationship between political ideas and theology, the famous German theologian, Karl Barth, described good politics as "parables of the Kingdom". By this he meant that political choices and programmes were to be illumined by a process of analogical imagination which moved from the gospel to the situation. Reflections on the miracle of reconciliation that is occurring in South Africa at present reverses the direction of this analogical procedure – a theological reading of the politics of the ANC in general, and Nelson Mandela in particular, now illuminates the gospel in a new way. For what is being practiced by Mandela can only be described as a politics of grace – grace in the full-blown, unadulterated sense of forgiveness and restoration that is undeserved, unmerited, and unearned.

But, as St. Paul was to discover in the misunderstandings that his message of God's free grace to recalcitrant sinners generated, grace is a notion which is fraught with difficulties: theological, ethical, and political. Grace can be and often is spurned, leaving the one who offers it feeling humiliated. Grace can be and often is adulterated into what Dietrich Bonhoeffer (a German theologian executed by the Nazi's after his participation in the plot to assassinate Hitler) called "cheap grace" – the acceptance of the offer of forgiveness and reconciliation without any reciprocal owning of responsibility and action. Bonhoeffer's words concerning this abuse of grace are apposite: "Cheap grace is the preaching of forgiveness without requiring repentance, baptism without church discipline, communion without confession, absolution without personal confession" (1960).

If, indeed, grace can be manipulated and abused in the theological and religious spheres, then there is no doubt that the same pertains in the political arena. But before looking at these problems, we must first grasp how grace is encountered today in the political arena.

It was, of all things, the rugby World Cup which initially prompted these reflections. Arriving back in South Africa after six years of study in the United States, I cleared customs at Johannesburg International Airport in the middle of the rugby World Cup final. Having kept abreast with local politics and sports via the Internet, I had heard that the World Cup, and in particular the performance of the Springboks, had gripped the imagination of the whole country. I must confess to having harboured a deep suspicion of these reports – after all, rugby, unlike other national sports, remains almost exclusively a white male preserve. I had also been home a few years earlier when, having been requested by the ANC not to sing the old national anthem and not to display the old South African flag, the sixty thousand spectators at the international match between the Springboks and the Wallabies had defied this request with a recidivist vengeance. Never before had the old flag been so extravagantly displayed, and the anthem was defiantly sung in the moment of silence that had been requested in memory of the victims of the Boiphatong massacre that had occurred only weeks before. Listening to the radio talk show discussions following this event, I remember being overwhelmed with a pessimism about the possibility of a resolution to the then political impasse. The political divide between white and black perceptions of the incident seemed to be an unbreachable chasm.

But that was then and this was now. In the interim the first democratic elections had occurred, the new flag had been unfurled to widespread acclaim, a compromise anthem had been crafted, and most importantly, a new President, Nelson Mandela, had been inaugurated.

One remembers, however, that in the months leading up to the World Cup tournament it had seemed as if rugby would again rend asunder the fragile sense of national unity. The rugby team, it was argued, was simply not representative of the "Rainbow nation". Raging debates over the Rugby Union's poor record in development programmes necessary to rectify the imbalances and injustices of apartheid, and bitter memories of the flag-waving defiance which had marred the previous international tours led many black South Africans to question the propriety of hosting the World Cup in South Africa. At very best, most black South Africans seemed to cultivate a studied disinterest in the whole affair as the tournament date approached.

One remembers too that the debate concerning the Springbok symbol had ignited passions to a fever pitch. The compromise which was reached by the rugby authorities and the National Sports Council had left everyone feeling annoyed. Many blacks felt that the Rugby Board were once again proving themselves unable to adapt to the new political realities, and many whites (with breathtaking historical amnesia), carped on about the 'interference of politicians in sport'.

Into this potentially explosive cauldron stepped the man whose political sensibilities have proved impeccable, whose understanding of the power of symbolic acts to make or break community surpasses the most canny of religious leaders, and whose insight into the power of grace to transform people and nations puts most theologians to shame. Mandela's visit to the South African team before the opening game set the process of the politics of grace in motion. In his television interview after the meeting, he stated that until 1994, he, along with most black people in the country, had always supported whichever team was opposing the Springboks. But now, he went on, he was urging everyone in the country, black and white, to unite behind "our boys". Standing beside him, the captain of the Springboks, a white Afrikaner, told the nation that the team were going to win the game "for our President".

This one simple act of political courage and gracious accommodation by the President turned the tide dramatically. It seemed as if the whole nation now swung behind the team*,

---

* A somewhat bemused black ANC Member of Parliament recounted how the next morning over the breakfast table she had stated to her son that despite what Madiba (Mandela) had said, she could not regard a team made up of whites as "our boys", only to be met with her son's retort: "But mom, they're our whites"!

and to everyone's surprise (except, so he claims, the President), the Springboks won the opening game convincingly. The spectacular vista of Newlands stadium awash in the colours of the new flag, gave one a palpable sense that the vision of the "Rainbow Nation" was receiving a new defining set of symbols.

The Springboks of course, eventually qualified for the finals, and almost the whole country was now united behind the team. Mandela, once more, showed his symbolic acumen. His appearance in the pre-game rituals of presenting the teams to the various dignitaries in the No. 6 rugby jersey of the Springbok captain was a stroke of genius. (He later wore the same jersey at an ANC rally in the townships and endorsed the continuing use of the Springbok as the rugby emblem.) In one simple act, he once more mobilised a symbolic logic of almost salvific power. The crowd (again, predominantly white and male), burst into a sustained chant of "Nelson, Nelson, Nelson", transferring to him the liminal energy usually reserved for the sporting icons. In this wonderfully graceful, but extremely insightful gesture, Mandela was able to channel the religious, psychic, and ritual energy to himself and to his vision of the nation. And as is now history, the Springbok team, inspired no doubt by this affirmation and by the support of the nation, went on to win the game, and hence the World Cup.

The cynic, of course, sees in this manipulation of symbols – their symbolic deconstruction and reconstruction – a crass mobilising of mass emotions for the sake of political projects. And, of course, there may be some of that in this move. Three things, however, undermine the cynic's suspicion. The first is the project to which these actions are directed – the reconstruction and reconciliation of one of the most divided, alienated, and violent societies, in which ethnic and cultural differences continue to threaten the fragile sense of nationhood which is emerging. The second is the man himself – Mandela has shown such a consistent integrity that few, if any, accuse him of hypocrisy. There is a substance to his acts that simply cannot be reduced to clever (or dumb) campaign politics. Third is the consistency of this "politics of grace" when it is politically unpopular. The rugby incident is just one of many instances of a pattern of reconciling grace that has been salvific for the country. They include the invitation to the wives of the former

State Presidents to tea with senior women of the ANC, and the quite remarkable visit Mandela paid to Betsie Verwoerd in the 'white' enclave of Orania.

But as I have already intimated, as even the Apostle Paul had discovered, such a practice of grace, in its very recklessness and profligate abundance, is not always received in the manner intended. Indeed, two very real dangers have emerged for the politics of grace which are very similar to theological understandings of the primacy of grace.

The first is the problem of resentment among those who feel that such grace is undeserved, unnecessarily extravagant and given too easily, that is, without the necessary quid pro quo being assured up front. Politically, those who have long been victims of the system of apartheid look with some understandable suspicion verging on disdain on the attempts made by the President to reconcile the former oppressor. They seem to border on an appeasement that undermines the legitimate anger and de-mands for retribution felt by many victims of apartheid. An analogy with the justified anger of the faithful brother of the Prodigal at his father's excessive grace towards his profligate brother is perhaps apt.

This danger is a valid one, and is fuelled by the second danger, which has to do with the reception of this grace. For, as the Epistle of James laments about the misuse of Paul's understanding of the faith-works dialectic, the miraculous grace which has been offered to white South Africans is too often misused, and is misused in such a way that the suspicions of the elder brother in the story of the Prodigal are confirmed. To be more specific: one continues to detect in radio talk-shows, in the conversations of families and friends, in newspaper articles and letters to the editor, a certain self-righteous carping about the new South Africa which usually begins with the statement: "I was never for apartheid, but ...", and which then goes on to list a litany of complaints about the decline of white privilege, couched in the general terms of 'declining standards'. In complaints about crime, about squatters, about the disruption of services through strike action, about corruption and fraud, there is very, very little self-reflection, let alone self-criticism, which sees in these horrendous social crises the legacy of white domination. Having so graciously been forgiven, having at tremen-dous political cost being offered a new place in the sun, it would often seem that this is interpreted as a carte blanche to criticise and condemn the new and fragile democracy. Instead of accepting the miracle of grace with humility, repentance, and a desire for conversion, too often this grace is treated as a right, as a natural product of a democracy.

At one's most irritated moments one wonders whether, in fact, this grace was given too easily, whether it has become Bonhoeffer's "cheap grace", demanding neither repentance nor the conversion of attitude and life which it seeks. Perhaps. But then the offer of grace always implies a risk that it will be spurned, that it will be abused. Why then take the risk? Because it is clear that its power to save, to transform, remains enormous. While retribution would have been satisfying for many, and would have clearly been more just, its consequences would have been horrific, not only for whites (who would have deserved all they got), but for the prospects of salvation for the whole nation.

It is here that the question of the Truth and Reconciliation Commission becomes so important to the life of the country and to the health of the body politic. For grace, daring and profligate as it is, requires a response. Grace spurned, grace abused, has consequences. It is this insight which is the basis for the biblical insistence on God's vengeance, or notions of final judgment and punishment that cannot be avoided in the Hebrew Bible and the New Testament alike. While God's continuing love and offer of salvation remain open even for the repentant criminal on the cross, it is impossible to be consistent to the biblical witness and ignore the multiple warnings of the dire consequences of spurning God's initiative of love. This does not mean, of course, that God changes from a forgiving to a revengeful deity. It is the insight of grace that we get what we deserve if we are, ultimately, punished. We deserve our condemnation, our sentence is warranted, and we have our just desserts. "But for grace" – and that is a big but – we should expect nothing less than punishment and condemnation.

It is grace, then, which offers a way out of the implacable inevitability of a justice understood as an exacting of vengeance in retribution, but does so by recasting justice in the form of a restitution which arises out of a response to forgiveness.

Biblically, the paradigmatic example of this process is that of Zacchaeus, the hated tax-collector to whom Jesus holds out the possibility of restoration. Zacchaeus's response is a demonstration of the true meaning of the justice of grace: he accepts the offer of forgiveness and reconciliation, and immediately undertakes to attempt to put right the many things he has done wrong, including the paying of restitution to his many victims. After hearing his response, Jesus exclaims: "Today salvation has come to this house!" (Lk 19:1-10). Justice by means of restitution is accomplished, but in a manner which effects reconciliation between victim and perpetrator.

It is apparent from the narrative that the story has two foci: the offer of grace to an oppressive member of a despised class by Jesus, and Zacchaeus's response. Both acts elicit amazement. That Jesus would go out of his way to speak to Zacchaeus, and, even more startling, offer to eat with him, created much dissent among Jesus' followers, among whom were surely victims of Zacchaeus's avarice and collaboration. But Jesus does not capitulate to the pressure of such dissent. "Amazing grace!" we might exclaim. But the story is only completed with an account of Zacchaeus's repentance and restitution. It is at this point that salvation comes, and Zacchaeus is reintegrated into the community: this man, too, is a son of Abraham (Lk 19:9). Thus grace creates the space for conversion of the oppressor, restitution to the victims, and reconciliation between the two. Quite clearly, the latter two are dependent on the former, but the former is only effective because of the latter.

The TRC is thus an essential element in the politics of grace. It is the time of judgment in which "each one may receive what is due to him or her for the things done while in the body" (II Cor. 5:10). It is a judgment, or an accounting, which will enable that which has been done in the dark to be exposed, so that the truth will be revealed. Jesus' commentary on the politics of oppression remains valid: "Everyone who does evil hates the light, and will not come into the light for fear that his [or her] deeds will be exposed" (John 3:20). Whatever the protests of those complicit in the horror of apartheid, whatever their desire to keep hidden that which has been done by them or in their name, such an accounting is necessary for the healing of the body politic to begin. For it must be understood by all of us who have benefited from apartheid that what was done in our name requires our accountability, our ownership.

But this "Truth" dimension of the TRC is set within the politics of grace, as undeserved and unwarranted as any divine offer of grace might be. It is not truth for its own sake which is being sought, important as that is. Rather, it is truth which is being sought within the parameters of reconciliation and forgiveness. The amnesty provisions make this point legally. The attitude of Mandela and Tutu make this point ethically, religiously.

Grace requires a response that is accountable, repentant, forthright and, in turn, forgiving. It requires above all a humility which recognises it for what it is – not some hard won political concession, but a magnanimous, profligate and undeserved bounty of forgiveness which can and must be grasped in gratitude.

Mandela's politics of grace is one of the theologically most remarkable political experiments in history. If it succeeds, it will have saved not only the country, but will offer a model of political praxis that will be paradigmatic for many other countries emerging from bitter strife and division. The TRC is perhaps the key component in making these politics ethically and politically effective.

BIBLIOGRAPHY

Bonhoeffer, D. 1960. *The Cost of Discipleship*. New York: Macmillan

Willa Boesak

Truth, Justice and Reconciliation

The weak long for revenge, but the strong seek justice – Anonymous

In my book *God's Wrathful Children* (1995) I proposed that the Government of National Unity should and must espouse an ethic of vengeance and retribution. For many this would sound totally out of place in a land with a President who is a living symbol of forgiveness and reconciliation. To be sure, the notion of vengeance conjures up the vision of revengeful black people who would like to destroy their former oppressors. Nothing is further from the truth. My assessment is that people at the grassroots level are very willing to forgive but not to forget so easily. The call "let's forget about the past and look to the future" mocks the plight of millions of people who still suffer because of the apartheid past. The gospel's predilection for the poor remains our criterion and not whether a few have gained new-found wealth via affirmative action or ride in the parliamentary gravy train. Let us therefore take a closer look at my proposal.

The Christian ethicist is faced with the standard argument that God alone has the exclusive right to judgmental and wrathful intervention. Normally Rom 12:19 is quoted: "Vengeance is mine, saith the Lord", but that is to ignore that the apostle Paul immediately thereafter admonishes that God's rightful avenger is none other than the civil authorities to punish evildoers (Rom 13:14). God is surely not without passion, and the experience of abject poverty elicits divine wrath. Third World theologians in the *Road to Damascus* document (1988) further discover the wrath of God in the wrath of the marginalised. It follows that the resolution of the poor's wrath is the resolution of God's wrath. The election of our first democratic government was crucial but that was merely the beginning of the transformation of South Africa/Azania, not the end. Upon it rests the responsibility to deal with the past effectively otherwise the anger and hurt of many would remain dangerously unresolved. Destructive black rage may well become a perennial societal problem, for the marginalised will not accept political changes that do not end chronically low wages, joblessness, bad housing, and inferior education.

Human vengeance is an ambiguous concept. It emanates from human anger, which often includes hatred and malice. Nevertheless, these feelings of vengeance cannot simply be dismissed as a destructive force, for it can be a valid basis for resistance. Thus concluded the Dutch theologian E. Smelik who felt compelled to grapple with the desire for vengeance during the Nazi occupation of the Netherlands (1940-45). If the differentiation between *wraak* (revenge, vengefulness, blind destructive fury, vindictiveness) and *vergelding* (recompense, requital, retribution, reward) is not maintained, a serious terminological devaluation takes place. While "vengeance" frequently serves to denote both, its distinct applications, *wraak* and *vergelding*, are not interchangeable. The former, Smelik argues, belongs in the sphere of senselessness, unkindness, unreasonableness and hate. Human vengeance, then, needs to be removed from the subjective, interpersonal sphere and brought to the objective control of a court of justice. It is in the juridical terrain that the mode of vengeance is morally manifested in the *vergelding* forms of recompense, requital, retribution, and reward.

The systematic fragmentation and polarisation of South Africans in terms of race, gender, tribe and class have led to hate and fear. The violence entrenched in our society seems senseless, but is in fact a consequence of centuries of colonial oppression, alienation and extended suffering. From a historical point of view, it is not surprising that a particular dimension of township upheavals is acts of vengeance by the dispossessed. These are not always forces of destruction. Understanding God's wrathful children in our context requires the ability to see within their deeds of despair and hear within their cries of rage the cry for justice. Many whites seem to expect black people not to succumb to bitterness, anger or aggression no matter how much they are exploited or traumatised. However, a kind of unnatural "Christian" patience and reasonableness vis-à-vis this history of misery is not Christian at all, but a distorted ethos of sub-missiveness. Are black people supposed to be happy living in the dirty and drab sameness of congested ghettos or poverty-stricken rural areas? Thus a lack of wrath in the face of injustice is actually a failure to care.

The President was therefore right to appoint the Truth and Reconciliation Commission. It would have been immoral to expect from the victims of torture or the bereaved to sweep their experiences under the floor mat. It is also a · necessary step toward that ultimate national goal: genuine reconciliation. However, I have one great concern, namely, that reconciliation will not and cannot be achieved without justice. Although the commission is not a tribunal, it should not guarantee blanket absolution and amnesty for all perpetrators. The crucial question is: when the truth is revealed, what then? To know who murdered Biko or Ford Calata without referring the information to the courts, will definitely not bring about reconciliation. I therefore suggest that two forms of justice be enacted.

The first is punitive or retributive justice. In modern times the moral dilemma of the relation among retributive justice, the Torah's demand of forgiveness (e.g. Gen 50:17, Lev 5:6-10) and forgiveness itself is illustrated by the continued hunting of Nazi criminals. Very recently French collaborator Paul Touvier was jailed for life. To be sure, the Israelis know well that the incarceration of an Eichmann or a Hess cannot be taken as satisfaction for six million Jews murdered in the gas chambers of Treblinka, Belsen, Maidanek and Auschwitz. Should the Jews not be asked to forget the trauma of the Holocaust? Should former SS officer Alois Brunner, henchman of Eichmann, who still lives in Damascus, Syria, not be "forgiven" so that he can die in peace?

The central issue emerging from this illustration is that of *accountability*. A theological ethic of vengeance and wrath cannot be built on a distorted notion of forgiveness in which the tie between punitive justice and the goal of reconciliation has been severed. Rather, such an ethic should consider the problems of accountability as it relates to the living experiences of the victims of political crime. Consider the "Trojan horse" method used in Athlone to lead pupils to their deaths. Who planned and ordered that? Consider what interrogator "Spyker" van Wyk told the Rev Cedric Mason: "I am not a Christian. I hate you and all your kind. I don't mind if I kill you."

In 1976 the UN declared that apartheid was a crime against *humanity*. That means that not only were the rights of individuals violated, but also of society at large. Therefore, whilst the stories and confessions before the commission are vital, a much broader ethical issue is at stake. The pent-up anger of the people must also be addressed and channelled in a constructive way. A court of law provides that responsible channel. At the funeral of Chris Hani the Young Lions carried a placard: "We will never forgive the murderers of Comrade Hani!" I'm not saying that every apartheid criminal should be indicted, but at least those at the top level who gave the orders. The Magnus Malans of this world cannot expect mercy. Neither can the quest for retributive justice be trivialised and reduced to a witch-hunt.

Secondly, the ethical maxim that corresponds to the quest for compensatory justice is reparation. An ethic of vengeance also concerns itself with vindicating the victims of South African Ku Klux Klanism and neo-Nazism. In Chile reparations (pensions) were granted to the bereaved. In order to hope for a renewed and transformed society, the victims in turn must shun vindictiveness and the desire to take revenge upon their former oppressors. It is equally imperative for a democratic, post-apartheid government to espouse justice and uphold courageously an ethic of vengeance, knowing that ultimately their judgement falls under the judgement of the eternal God.

The work of this commission will cost us, the tax payers and the donors, millions of rands. It will be unacceptable if the element of justice is vitiated and the whole process becomes a superficial exercise.

SELECT BIBLIOGRAPHY
Boesak, W. 1995. *God's Wrathful Children*. Grand Rapids
ICT. 1988. *The Road to Damascus*. Cape Town
Mayson, C. 1984. *A Certain Sound*. New York
Smelik, E. 1941. *Wraak, Vergelding en Vergeving*. 's-Gravenhage

Molefe Tsele

Kairos and Jubilee

Introduction

1994 will go down in the annals of our country as the year of liberation, when *de jure* apartheid ended, ushering in a new era of freedom and democratic rule in South Africa. It was with that historical backdrop in mind that the Second International Kairos Conference was held in Johannesburg in September 1995 to celebrate the Tenth Anniversary of the 1985 Kairos Document and to ponder the question: "Are we facing a new kairos in 1995?"

What was expected to be a triumphant gathering of theologians who were individually and collectively persecuted and suffered for their prophetic witness against apartheid was tempered by a sense of sadness that the reality of our vision of liberation fell far short of our expectations. One report after another of the prevailing conditions for the majority of the masses seemed to indicate troubling trends. The words "helplessness", "despair", "frustration", seemed to punctuate every report and thereby deny any sense of celebration of the new era.

It is this mixture of celebration of the new under the ominous shadow of the past that will constitute the theme of this essay on Kairos and Jubilee. Our faith in the future is being tested to its limits. It is now, more than at any other time, that we need to affirm as a matter of faith, rather than on the basis of objective facts, that the new has arrived in the midst of the old. We recall in this connection Jesus standing in the midst of the synagogue at the beginning of his ministry and reading the scripture quoting the Prophet Isaiah 61:

The Spirit
of the Sovereign Lord is on me,
because the Lord has anointed me
to preach good news to the poor.
He has sent me ...
to proclaim the year of the Lord's favour ...

For most of his audience, this proclamation encapsulated their lifelong dream of liberation, and possibly this text formed one of the favourite canons of the time, especially as they were experiencing colonial occupation and oppression. But the punch line of the text comes a little later when Jesus said: "Today this scripture has been fulfilled in your hearing" (Luke 4:21).

To make this claim in the midst of the old order must have seemed Utopian, since the objective facts pointed to the contrary. But here Jesus was making an affirmation of faith and stating the obvious.

In like manner, we need to test the significance of our time and our new democracy, and ask in spite of the litany of social ills that have followed in its wake, whether we can say that something new, opportune, creative and authentic is taking place here; and further that, unless we grasp the moment, we may risk relapsing into a worse tyranny than we have known. This is to ask the kairos-jubilee question.

What is Our Kairos Today?

Perhaps the best way to describe the characteristic features of our times is to look at the overarching, enduring, systemic factors, rather than focusing on the episodic. The dominant feature of our time is a system that has gained universal appeal as the only "rational" alternative, namely, the neo-liberal free market system. The situation is further complicated by the fact that a case can be made for the attractiveness of the system. However, the fundamental logic of this system, even in its apparent irreplaceability, is that it requires sacrifices for its success. Even more disturbing is the fact that it tends to feed on the poor and weak members of the

71

community. The calculus of costs seem to allocate more sacrifices to the poor while those who are privileged and affluent reap the rewards of the system. The pauperisation inherent is not temporary nor equitable, on the contrary, it is systemic and places an unjustifiable burden on the poor and weak members of society. It is in this context that we choose to reflect on the kairotic features of our present situation.

First, there seems to be a dearth of idealism. The system's triumph has killed any aspiration and yearning for alternatives. It seems to tell us that there is no other alternative. The lesson of history has pronounced an unequivocal judgement and declared this to be the only alternative. In that respect, the blunt message seems to be: if you are in search of the future, this is it. The tragedy is that, if this is the content of the future, for a majority of the people this is bad news. Based on what we have seen, we remain unimpressed.

Second, there seems to be a deep disappointment with and sense of betrayal by a liberation project that is incapable of engaging this system. In trying to make a deal with the system, perhaps out of necessity, the liberation movement has been left with an illusion at best, and a sham sense of power at worst. The reality seems to indicate that the system has managed to change one partner or servant of power for another. Previously, it needed and used the apartheid regime for its interests, now it conveniently uses the democratic forces, in spite of the resistance of the latter and their good intentions. Of course, this is not to say that the democratic forces are used by the system surreptitiously. Our point is that they cannot help it. The ubiquity of the system leaves them with no option on the matter. There is thus a new realisation that real power does not lie with our elected officials, but is located somewhere else. The tragedy is that here, power is not accountable to the electorate, but to shareholders. Our cherished dream of democracy turns out to be a fraud. We believed in the ballot but nobody told us that we should rather invest our power in the stock market. The new message seems to be: forget about the vote, what matters are the shares. Real power is negotiated at the stock exchange and not in parliament. Finally, the system seems to be victorious in the values market. We are witnessing the emergence of a new global cultural value system premised on consumption and economic growth. The growing destruction of natural resources, loss of the reverence for life and nature, the breakdown of moral and social fabric, the growing culture of violence and unapologetic cut-throat competition for profit, seem to be the logical stepchildren of this system. What we are lamenting in South Africa today, namely, car-jacking crimes, white-collar crimes, endemic corruption in big business and government sectors, crimes against women and children, are products of this culture of unlimited profit maximisation at all costs. The new creed seems to be: You count if you have, you don't count if you don't have. How else can we explain the policies that wish to guarantee ill-gotten property and reward criminals while being ready to ask for patience from victims and even forget those who sacrificed their youth for liberation? The shame of our liberation is that it readily forgets the memory of its martyrs while bending over backwards to assuage the fears of former villains.

It will be a double tragedy if we fail to perceive the creative opportunity offered by this very moment. The greatest challenge is to be able to proclaim God's continuing liberatory work even in the midst of this despair. The mere willingness to describe our present situation of new-found freedom in kairotic language is itself an acknowledgement of the fundamental crisis for which we are heading, and it implies a confession that something better is demanded of us and is possible in our history. Our affirmation of the kairos is therefore simultaneously a call for the jubilee of God. It is the refusal of our human spirit to succumb to the finality of history and to the absoluteness of any one particular system, however popular and successful it may have proved. The path from kairos should lead to jubilee.

At the Threshold of Jubilee
On the Day of Atonement
you shall have the trumpet sounded throughout all your land.
And you shall hallow the fiftieth year
and you shall proclaim liberty throughout the land
to all its inhabitants.
It shall be a jubilee for you:
you shall return, everyone of you, to your property
and everyone of you to your family.
(Leviticus 25: 9-10)

Drafted towards the end of the exile in Babylon, the author of Leviticus was preoccupied with the difficult task of resettlement, rebuilding and reconstruction that lay ahead. He envisioned the new order to be established in the new land to be founded in the spirit of the Lord's Sabbath and Jubilee. For the Israelites, Jubilee was more than simple return from exile to a former state, but restoration to a new and better state. A return from the Babylonian slavery into a free Israel, without the resources and opportunities to lead a free life, would only result in their relapse into new debts and new slavery, only this time they would have exchanged one master for another.

Thus Jubilee is a new lease of life, an opportunity to begin anew and avoid the errors of the past that led into debt, slavery and loss of their land in the first place. Those who had gone into exile, had become landless, were in bondage or indebted, had to receive restitution, forgiveness of debts and reclamation of their lost dignity. What they had lost was not simply material possessions such as property and land, but the very essence of their humanity, their self-esteem, human dignity, identity, culture, religion. We can say they had lost their ubuntu, and Jubilee is all about that: the reclamation of ubuntu both individually and communally.

But it is also more. It is an attempt to institutionalise the spirit of Jubilee so that it can become a permanent and ongoing feature of the new order, the model for a new social and economic relationship whose objective is to ensure that no one falls permanently into a state of bondage. It especially ensures that the descendants of those who do so fall are not themselves destined to a life of the permanent underclass, due to the misfortune of their common ancestor.

What does this mean for us in South Africa today as we attempt to restructure our past and rebuild a new nation? What is the contextual meaning of Jubilee for the task of nation rebuilding? It would seem that the concrete reality of Jubilee has to be defined with respect to the kairotic challenge of reconstructing both the socio-economic landscape and moral "soulscape" of our country. This implies embarking on an ambitious programme and process of correcting the past imbalances: reconciliation of victims and victimisers to restore the broken community, restoration of our lost human dignity and ubuntu, the rebuilding of our broken nation.

While this process will remain an Utopia in the present conditions of history, we affirm our faith that the foundations of such a Jubilee can be constructed in history. Like the returning Israelites, we confess that the God of Jubilee is actively involved to liberate us from bondage of every strand and urges us to be involved in this task.

We can identify four important processes in our country at present which seek to give a historical realisation of the Jubilee spirit in our time. These are: the Truth and Reconciliation Commission (TRC), the Reconstruction and Development Programme (RDP), Affirmative Action Programme (AA) and the Nation Building Project.

The Truth and Reconciliation Commission

The stated objective of the TRC, namely, the promotion of national reconciliation and unity, mirrors what the Jubilee message promotes. In that spirit, the TRC will be undermining this ideal if it degenerates into a "Nuremberg" style inquisition into the past. However, for the TRC to be an authentic organ that promotes healing and restoration, the question of justice needs to be addressed. The fear that the TRC may be an easy and painless option for the guilty to be exonerated without due regard to the victims is not unfounded.

One cannot overlook the fact that most of the human rights offenders have always seen the TRC as a threat, and some continue to oppose it unless they get guarantees that it will not lead to their culpability. Indications are that insofar as the TRC seeks to give such guarantees, it may become injurious to victims of past human rights abuses.

Our view is that if it is to realise its stated objectives, the TRC must above all seek the restoration of the humanity of both the victims and offenders. It must accord indemnity on the basis of the genuine confession and even willingness on the part of the offender to face prosecution.

Confession on condition of immunity still falls short of the confession of someone who has come to realise that he had fallen below his/her ubuntu. It is such a person who must be met halfway by the assurance that his past will not be held against him, and thus be declared forgiven. The absolute minimum requirement for the TRC is voluntary and full disclosure of the past crime.

As regards the victims, due consideration should be given to the material resources and opportunities that should be made available for them to rebuild their lives. The comforting knowledge that the offender has been exposed, while it is cathartic on its own, is not, however, sufficient. The Jubilee spirit requires that those who were in bondage be placed in a position to rebuild their lives.

It is critical, therefore, that the commissioners be preferentially disposed to the victims rather than the offenders. Here we support the call for the moral distinction between the oppressed and oppressors in the examination of human rights abuses. This is the Jubilee for those who were in bondage and not for the slave masters. One can assume that as former exiles returned to reclaim their lost land, the present owners were not celebrating. The Jubilee of the Lord was good news to the oppressed, captives, slaves.

The Reconstruction and Development Programme

The RDP is an ambitious national programme aimed at correcting past imbalances and the transformation of the apartheid socio-economic life, in order to make it responsive to those who were previously excluded and disadvantaged. Its overall programme is aimed at empowerment, capacity building of communities, provision of infrastructure and basic life essentials, and the rebuilding of broken communities. It builds on the realisation that once apartheid laws have gone, people's lives do not automatically change. Those who were held in bondage for generations will face the same lot even after the dawn of liberation. The RDP is an acknowledgement of this challenge and an attempt to redress it by social engineering mechanisms, rather than leave it to the system to self-correct according to its own mechanisms.

Evidence emerging shows that people's lives at the bottom heap of society have not only continued to be a struggle, but have in some areas, such as farming, become worse since the 1994 elections. In general, the material conditions of many people are worsening. The RDP is a vehicle to arrest this continuing decline of living conditions, and also to empower those previously oppressed to rebuild their conditions.

Here again, a critical question needs to be directed into all RDP programmes: whom do they benefit? The logic of our economic system, as we have argued, will tend to benefit the rich at the expense of the poor. It will not be accidental that a programme purporting to help the poor in actual fact ends up becoming another feasting ground for the rich. In this respect, an audit of the RDP must be periodically conducted to test the programme. We are making a case for a RDP that is unapologetic in its preferential option for the upliftment of the material conditions of the poor.

Affirmative Action Policies

There is lack of clarity in the ongoing debate about affirmative action policies. Some decry them as reverse racism at worst, or discrimination at best. In our view, it is an affront to any rules of fair-play and sense of justice to expect those who were disadvantaged to compete with those who had a head start by virtue of the benefits they enjoyed from their position of privilege. The Jubilee imperative requires that those who have been excluded through no fault of their own but simply at the whim of government policies, cannot now be asked to compete in the free market of opportunities with others. What affirmative action policies seek to achieve is a structural correction of this historical imbalance in order to give the disadvantaged a chance of succeeding. It is premised on the conviction that when left to its own, the system will tend to favour those who are favourably positioned and those who have historically benefited. In this connection too, we affirm policies that adopt preferential treatment for those who were historically disadvantaged.

Within the Jubilee understanding, this entails enabling them to transform their position of vulnerability and weakness to become authentically free. We remain cautious and critical, however, of affirmative action policies that perpetuate the victim mentality and the entitlement culture. When properly construed, affirmative action policies should be liberatory and transformative. There must be a clear intention to seek the full empowerment of those historically discriminated against.

77

Nation Building: A New Koinonia

The call for Jubilee is a call for a new community defined by new value systems and social relationships. For us in South Africa, this task is linked to the project of redefining for ourselves our new identity as a nation, different from anything previously known in our history. South Africa is both symbolically, legally and sociologically rebuilding itself – literally from the ruins of its past. This could and can be seen in multiple ways: in the debates about the new National Flag and National Anthem; the process of drafting the New Constitution; and generally the yearning for identity in sports, academia, mass media and elsewhere.

The pertinent question is, how do we choose to define ourselves, or by what values and symbols do we wish to be identified? Here the concept of *koinonia* becomes a companion symbol to describe the content of a Jubilee community. A *koinonia* is a community that is founded above all on the values of mutuality and co-operation. In this community, every member is first and foremost a fellow human person and sister or brother. Here, the values of ubuntu are espoused. This is what nation building requires as we go through a process of healing and reconciliation.

Conclusion

Professor Bonganjalo Goba in his commemoration address at the tenth anniversary celebration of the Kairos Document at Regina Mundi, Soweto, observed that our situation seems to be destined to fail a majority of our people and sentence them to the permanent status of the underclass. We have argued that there is something fundamentally wrong with the basic orientation of our system, and that inherent within its apparent triumph are the sacrifices of the poor and weak members of our society. We have affirmed our faith in the challenge and opportunity that is presented by this system to pursue the task of realising God's Jubilee in history.

Wolfram Kistner

The Biblical Understanding of Reconciliation

Reconciliation in the Letter of Paul

The term which the Greek New Testament uses for reconciliation occurs only in the letters of Paul. It occurs only five times. On the other hand, he uses it in contexts which are of crucial significance for understanding his interpretation of the Gospel.

From my reading of the letters of Paul, I have come to the conclusion that his basic religious insights and discovery arose from his experience that in Christ believers of Jewish and of Gentile background can live together in peace as a new community. Hostilities are being overcome in this community which otherwise are considered to be irreconcilable in society (Eph 2:14-22).

What generally is described as Paul's conversion was the experience of a calling to become an apostle in terms of a broader idea of the people of God which comprises people of Jewish and of Gentile background (Rom. 11:11-16). Believers of Jewish background are not expected to give up their Jewish traditions in this community (Gal 3:6-14). On the contrary, the broadening of the notion of the people of God so as to comprise also people of other backgrounds is in line with the most precious promises which God has given to the people of Israel (Gal 3:6-14). Neither are people of Gentile background who join this new community expected to live according to the traditions of the Jewish religion. Both Jews and Gentiles are accepted by

79

God by grace through Christ. The Church as the new community is meant to be an alternative society anticipating the healing of humankind and of the cosmos that has been disrupted by the effort of humans to discard their responsibility to their Creator. To Paul, resistance against this new fellowship is resistance against the unconditional acceptance of humans by God. In this context he emphasises what we generally describe as justification by faith – a concept that has become extremely individualised in the tradition of Protestant churches ever since the Reformation.

Paul's concern about justification by faith can only be understood in the context of his experience of God's reconciliation in Christ that comprises and has extended to the whole human community and to creation. It comprises even people who are not aware of it. From a Christian perspective it is the basis of efforts of people to bring about reconciliation in human relationships, of forgiving one another and of love of the enemy. We can resist God's reconciliation, but we cannot undo it. *In Christ* the foundation has been laid for people to live together as a *contrast society*, not separate from the world.

The key term through which Paul expresses the religious experience that underlies his calling to be an apostle is the word *reconciliation*. It implies the removal of hostilities and the restoration of fellowship, of peace. It indicates wholeness and healing and therefore is close to the Hebrew term *shalom*. At the time of Paul the Greek term "reconciliation" was mostly used to describe the act of humans to restore community and communication between enemies. In Paul's letters God himself is the initiator of such reconciliation. God initiates such reconciliation by entering our situation disrupted by self-centeredness and strife as a human in Christ. Through Christ we are placed in the midst of the struggles and strife that disrupt human relationships into a sphere in which such reconciliation can happen.

In 2 Cor 5:19 Paul states: *God was in Christ and reconciled the world to himself.* The universal and cosmic reconciliation *in Christ* thus has already happened. It comprises believers and non-believers and includes also our enemies. On the other hand people have to be invited to avail themselves of this reconciliation. Therefore Paul pleads: *We beseech you on behalf of Christ, be reconciled to God* (2 Cor 5:20). This appeal pertains to our acceptance of the reconciliation with God as well as to our acceptance of the reconciliation which God has brought about through Christ between us and our enemies. People who accept this reconciliation now already are part of God's new creation: *Therefore if anyone is in Christ, he is a new creation* (II Cor 5:17).

The experience of God's reconciliation in Christ that has already happened and that comprises all humans and creation obliged Paul to take an uncompromising stand against members of the Church who were anxious to establish barriers of irreconcilability in the Church (for instance, those in Galatia). At the same time it exposed him to persecution by religious leaders of the Jewish religious community as well as by the Roman Empire. The story of the collection of the Christian congregations in Macedonia illustrates the commitment which this understanding of God's comprehensive reconciliation requires from the Christian. The collection story also illustrates the economic and political relevance of such reconciliation.

In 1965 the German theologian Dieter Georgi wrote a book on the collection organised by the apostle Paul in the congregations of Macedonia. He taught theology for many years in the United States and was deeply influenced by the Civil Rights Movement, the Black Consciousness Movement and Liberation Theology. This book did not attract much attention at that time. Recently he has revised it in the light of new theological research on the issue of economic justice in the Bible. The revised version of the book has been published in German; the translated title is: *To remember the poor – The collection of Paul for Jerusalem* (1994).

Paul writes about the collection in the congregations of Macedonia in 2 Corinthians 8 and 9. These were congregations mainly of Gentile background. He mentions this collection also in the letter to the Christians in Rome (Rom 16:22-23). Probably the majority of the Christians in Rome at the time were of Jewish background. Paul tells the Christians in Rome that he is anxious to visit them and then to proceed from them to Spain in order to proclaim the Gospel also in that remote region. Before he comes to Rome he wants to deliver the collection personally in Jerusalem. He indicates to the Christians in Rome that the Christians in Jerusalem of Jewish background may not be willing to accept the collection from the Christians in Macedonia.

A widely accepted explanation for the tensions that existed between Paul and the Christians of Jewish background in Jerusalem is the following: they, as the respected custodians of the Christian faith in the oldest Christian congregation, distrusted Paul's understanding of his mission to the Gentiles. In particular, they distrusted his insistence that the Gentile Christians were to be incorporated into the people of God without being placed under an obligation to be circumcised and to follow Jewish religious traditions. According to this explanation Paul hoped that the love and faith of the Gentile Christians that manifested itself in the collection would legitimate his understanding of mission and of the Church in their eyes.

Georgi's research, however, has brought to light new aspects of the collection which explain in greater detail the seriousness of the tension between Paul and the Jewish Christians in Jerusalem (1994:87-89). Georgi finds evidence in the Bible which suggests that Paul intended to take a whole delegation of uncircumcised Christians of Gentile background with him to Jerusalem. Such a delegation from diverse Gentile nations was to remind the Christians in Jerusalem of the prophecies in the Holy Scriptures about the pilgrimage of the nations to Jerusalem which was to inaugurate a new phase in the history of the people of God. Paul's visit to Jerusalem with the delegation of uncircumcised Gentiles was to announce the fulfilment of this prophecy. The representatives of the Gentile nations would bring the gifts of the Gentile nations to Jerusalem. However their gift would not be deposited in the temple. It would be brought to the poor, the Christians, in Jerusalem, to the marginalised members of the followers of Jesus who at any rate were a despised and marginal group. According to Paul's planning of the visit of the delegation, the salvation of the Gentiles who brought the collection to Jerusalem was intended to provoke faith on the part of the Jews. This outlook of Paul was bound to offend the Jews and their religious leaders in Jerusalem. It would imply that the official religious leadership in Jerusalem was not representing the authentic faith of the people of God.

According to Georgi's research findings, Paul planned his visit to Jerusalem as a provocative eschatological demonstration. It was intended by Paul to be provocative in the same way as the symbolic actions of the prophets were often intended to be provocative. Paul hoped that this demonstration might provoke people of the Jewish religious community to join the Christian community which represented the *whole of Israel* comprising people of Jewish and of Gentile background. Georgi suggests that Paul may have had the tradition of the Jubilee year in mind when he wrote to the Corinthians about the collection.

If this was Paul's intention, the collection was meant to manifest the dawning of the age in which peace and justice were beginning to be restored in the people of God as the beginning of bringing justice and peace and reconciliation to the whole human community.

We know that Paul was not in a position to carry out his carefully planned eschatological demonstration in Jerusalem. Enemies aiming to take his life forced him to make detours on his journey to Jerusalem. Nevertheless, he carried out part of his plan. According to Georgi, the alarm which he caused among the Jewish Christians as well as in the Jewish religious community in general and the attention this alarm received on the part of the Roman authorities were the indirect cause of his arrest in Jerusalem. They were also the indirect cause of the further events that followed: the journey of Paul to Rome as a prisoner and ultimately his execution in Rome.

Recently a Jewish philosopher by the name of Jacob Taubes has added further insights to the interpretation of Paul's collection journey to Jerusalem. According to Taubes, Paul's theology is deeply rooted in Jewish tradition. Paul was a zealot who protested against the adaptation of the Jewish faith by the religious leaders of the upper classes to Roman-Hellenistic culture and expectations. Such adaptation tended to neutralise resistance against the oppressive rule of the Roman Empire. For this reason Paul describes himself as the delegate of the crucified Jesus Christ who has been raised from the dead and been entrusted with the highest authority and power by God. For Paul the crucified Jesus Christ who has risen from death is the Anti-Caesar. The Gospel of Jesus Christ paved the way for a universalism that differed radically from the universalism of the Roman Empire and that overthrew the value system promoted by Roman Hellenistic culture. It affirmed the faith of Israel but did so in Paul's sense of the faith of the whole of Israel which included the Christians of Gentile background.

The reflections of Jacob Taubes have been published in a book, *The Political Theology of Paul* (1993). Taubes highly appreciated the research findings of Dieter Georgi on the history of the collection of Paul. At the same time he argued that Georgi had not provided a satisfactory answer to one decisive question: why should the Christians of Jewish background in Jerusalem have been so alarmed at the visit of Paul bringing a collection from the Gentile congregations together with a delegation of Christians from diverse Gentile nations? In providing an answer to this question, Taubes points out that no clear-cut distinction between Jewish Christians in Jerusalem and the general Jewish community existed at the time when Paul wrote his letters. The city of Jerusalem had not as yet been destroyed. Jewish Christians worshipped together with other Jews in the temple and regarded themselves as members of that community. They benefited from the protection which was granted to the faith of Jewish religious community in the Roman Empire as an officially tolerated faith *(religio licita)*. They could reckon that they were reasonably safe and would probably not be persecuted as long as they were regarded by the authorities as part of the Jewish religious community.

This protection which the Jewish Christians in Jerusalem enjoyed would be seriously jeopardised if they engaged in any activities which distinguished them openly from the Jewish faith. According to Taubes the official leaders of the Jewish religious community were equally concerned that they would not disturb the relative peace they enjoyed as an officially recognised religion. Taubes maintains that their interpretation of the Torah was deeply influenced by the concern that they did not cause any irritation to public order and arouse the suspicion of the Roman authorities. According to his view this was exactly the theology from which Paul distanced himself.

These findings of theological research and theological discussion are still controversial. They have not been adequately tested. I do, however, suggest that there are sufficient indications which support the following outline of a framework for the interpretation of Paul's message of reconciliation.

Paul's message of the comprehensive reconciliation of God with the world in Christ, which has already happened and which is to be implemented by his Church, is a highly provocative message of the Church as an alternative society that obliges her to practise participation of all its members and sharing of its resources in its own life as well as in its relationship with the whole human community of which it is a part. At the same time this message places on the Church the obligation to take up the struggle against all structures and practices of irreconcilability in her own life and in society. This obligation pertains not merely to tensions arising from different cultural or religious traditions or racial differences. It pertains in particular to tensions arising from economic injustice and disparities. Moreover this message is bound to involve the Church in conflicts and often even expose her to hatred and persecution. Nevertheless the life of this alternative society and the message and practice of reconciliation entrusted to her is intended by God to give hope to the whole human community and to creation.

In terms of this understanding Paul's theology and his emphasis on God's comprehensive reconciliation in Christ with the world has far-reaching implications for the contribution which churches and their members have to make by virtue of their faith to justice in society.

Any effort to understand Paul's message of God's reconciliation in Christ with the world as the core of his proclamation of the Gospel cannot avoid the question of how this interpretation of the Gospel is related to the ministry and the message of Jesus.

The Jubilee Tradition in the Ministry of Jesus

Just as the emphasis on God's comprehensive reconciliation in Christ is an important key to the understanding of Paul's theology, the tradition of the Jubilee Year is an important key to the understanding of the ministry of Jesus and his announcement that the kingdom of God has entered our situation in him.

The Jubilee tradition has to be traced back to the effort of the Jews who had remained behind in the devastated land of Judea when the ruling class was deported to Babylonia to set up a Torah republic with a strict commitment to Yahweh's insistence on justice to all the members of the people. It focused attention particularly on economic justice and protected the smaller landowners against permanent enslavement and the loss of their land to the bigger landowners. These landowners tended to use their privileged position to accumulate more and more land and power. According to the Jubilee tradition every fiftieth year was to be a Jubilee year in which economic justice was restored. People who had lost their freedom as a result of debt slavery were to be released and the land which they had lost as a result of indebtedness was to be returned to them.

The Jubilee Year was announced on the Day of Atonement at the beginning of the Passover festival with the blowing of a special trumpet. The setting of the announcement of the Jubilee in the Atonement Day was an acknowledgement of the sinfulness inherent in the accumulation of wealth in the hands of a few which had to be rectified again and again.

The special nature of the Jubilee tradition of the Jewish post-exilic community becomes clearer if one tries to understand it against the background of the practice of the monarchs in the ancient Empires of the Near East under whose domination the people of Israel had to suffer for many centuries. They followed a policy of subjugating more and more peoples at the margins of their empire, exacting tribute from them in return for a degree of protection which they offered them against their enemies. They accumulated more and more land and wealth that was extorted from the subjugated nations. The rulers of these subjugated nations used to place the burden of the tribute to be paid to the Emperor and the additional contributions to be paid by their subjects for their own rule on the smaller landowners. This practice had the result that more and more of the smaller landowners became indebted to the bigger landowners and ultimately lost their land and their freedom. On particular occasions such as the accession of a new monarch to the throne of an ancient empire he would grant reprieve from burdens that had been imposed on subject nations. Such a measure was to give hope to the oppressed people that conditions would change and that the pressures put on them would be eased. The temporary alleviation of burdens served the purpose of averting the danger of rebellion at a time when the power base of the new ruler had not as yet been consolidated.

In a long-term perspective, however, the objective of such amnesties granted by the rulers of ancient Empires in the Near East was to consolidate their power base with the view to continuing oppression and exploitation. In contrast the Jubilee tradition in the people of Israel was not an act of grace on the part of a ruler. It was the manifestation of the concern of Yahweh, the God of the Covenant, for justice to be meted out to all people, in particular of his concern for the liberation and freedom of the poorer sections of the people and for the containment of the greed of the ruling class.

According to Luke 4:14-21 Jesus announced the kingdom of God that has entered our situation through himself as the beginning of God's Jubilee Year that would bring freedom to the prisoners, relief to the poor, healing to the sick and joy and new life to all marginalised members of the people of God. At the same time Jesus relied on his followers as the Jubilee people who were called by God to implement the kingdom of God and to give hope to the world. People who had hitherto been regarded and treated as objects by the powerful were now subjects who were held responsible for passing on the freedom and the gifts which God imparts to his people.

In the ministry of Jesus the Jubilee tradition has a very strong connotation of economic justice and of the obligation to share resources. This is evident in the parable of the servant who receives remission of his debt from his master but is not prepared to forgive the debt of his fellow servant (Mat 18:21-35). This parable pertains to the issue of how much a believer owes forgiveness to his or her fellow human being. Such forgiveness in general concerns the attitude of the believer towards the fellow human beings in all spheres of life. It includes the dimension of remitting debts of people who have become financially indebted to us. The same observation applies to the fifth petition in the Lord's Prayer according to the text of Matthew 6: *And forgive us our debts as we forgive those who have become our debtors.* According to this petition no disciple of Jesus may expect God's forgiveness if he or she insists on keeping a fellow human being in financial bondage.

Involvement in the struggle for economic justice and for freedom and respect of human dignity thus is an integral dimension of life of the believer who lives in fellowship with the risen Lord. In the announcement of the kingdom of God by Jesus the Jubilee tradition pertains not merely to the redistribution of resources and the restoration of the freedom of the people of God every fiftieth year. It also pertains to the daily life of the Christian. Every day the Christian is to draw strength from the amnesty brought about by God through Jesus and every day the believer is bound to pass on this amnesty to fellow human beings.

Already during the ministry of Jesus particular aspects and incidents in his proclamation of the Gospel and particular symbolic actions indicate that the Jubilee amnesty which he pronounced was bound to be extended beyond the limits of the people of Israel.

The message of the comprehensive reconciliation of God in Christ was the great contribution of the apostle Paul through which he placed the Gospel of Jesus into the setting of the Hellenistic cities and the Roman Empire and paved the way for the expansion of the Christian faith and its penetration into different countries and cultures.

The Implications of the Biblical Understanding of Reconciliation for the Administration of Justice

In Protestant churches one can distinguish between two different approaches to the issue of the relationship between the Biblical concept of reconciliation and the administration of justice:

1. The widely prevailing classical approach assumes that reconciliation in Christ and forgiveness pertain to the direct relationship between believers and God and also to the personal relationship between believers and their fellow human beings, but have no relevance to the administration of justice in society. In society and in the state law and order has to prevail in terms of God's concern to protect life against sin and destruction. The offender has to suffer punishment for his offence.
2. The second approach places the emphasis on the kingdom of God that has entered our lives through Christ and is relevant to all dimensions of human life and of Creation.

The two differing approaches to the understanding of the relationship between the Gospel and justice in public life share certain common convictions: through Christ all our sins are forgiven before God. The evildoer has been accepted by God, but not, however, his or her evil deed. God's forgiveness separates the evildoer from his deed. Even the criminal retains his or her dignity before God and continues to be loved by God.

The differences between the two approaches pertain particularly to the understanding of the punishment of the offender:

1. According to the classical approach the offender has to be punished for his or her sin in order to be able to make atonement for his or her offence. This insistence on punishment of the offender as a means of atonement is often justified by the argument that one has to distinguish between the personal responsibility of the individual believer in which love has to prevail and the official responsibility in public life in which the principles of law and order have to prevail.
2. In terms of the kingdom of God approach, God's reconciliation with the world in Christ is valid for all dimensions of life. Whether or not punishment should be meted out is to be determined by the careful consideration of how reconciliation and healing can best be promoted in the life of the offender as well as of the victim. The concern for reconciliation should also determine the type of response to an offence that is meted out to an offender. The second approach offers scope for renouncing punishment in terms of an amnesty as long as such response serves the purpose of reconciliation.

In the struggle against the apartheid system South African churches have resorted on two occasions to Paul's message of God's reconciliation with the world in Christ as the foundation of their resistance against the state: in the *Message to the People* of South Africa of 1968 and in the *Belhar Confession* of the DRC Mission Church of 1982.

In their approach to issues of justice in society many South African Christians hold the view that punishment has to be meted out to offenders according to the principle of atonement. This is evident if one considers the wide support which capital punishment receives from the public in South Africa. However, the validity of the classical approach with the clear-cut distinction between private and public responsibility of a Christian is highly questionable. Jesus' insistence on love of the neighbour including love of the enemy has implications not only for the private responsibility of the Christian but also for his or her responsibility in public life.

From the perspective of the Christian understanding of God's comprehensive reconciliation any punishment that is meted out to an offender and any amnesty that is granted is based on the following presuppositions:

1. The aim of punishment as well as the aim of an amnesty is to reintegrate the offender into society and at the same time to heal the wounds of the victims;
2. If under certain conditions it is found necessary to mete out punishment to the offender, the aim is to separate him or her from his or her offence and to liberate the person concerned from bondage to the offence and its consequences;
3. The potential for the abuse of power of which the offender has become guilty is also alive in the victims if they come to power;
4. The society and the religious or ideological community or cultural group which has contributed towards shaping the mind of the offender shares in the responsibility of the offence and is in need of repentance on its part and forgiveness on the part of God and the victims with the view to facilitating a process of healing and taking precautions against a repetition of the offence.

The Amnesty Issue in a Situation of Transition to Democracy
The English word amnesty is derived from a Greek verb pertaining to forgetting. A clear distinction is, however, necessary between amnesty and amnesia. The latter word is derived from the same root as amnesty. An amnesty refers to a deliberate act of forgetting after an offence has been brought to light and made known. It is not the offence which is forgotten, but the offender. A distinction is made between the offender and the offence. The person of the offender is allowed to be made forgotten through an amnesty in his capacity as an offender. The offence is, however, not allowed to be forgotten. On the contrary, the memory of the offence is retained in order to avoid a repetition of the offence and in order to respect the human dignity of the victims of the offence.

Amnesia, on the other hand, pertains to the loss of memory or in our context to the deliberate or the unconscious suppression of the memory of the offence by the offender or by the society of which he or she is a member. Such amnesia inhibits the process of healing in the life of the offender and can have the effect of causing bitterness among the victims of the offence. Possibly it can even stimulate acts of retribution and of further violence.

In the course of recent history the understanding and application of amnesties have undergone changes. Prior to World War I monarchs of West European countries still continued the tradition of the Jubilee amnesty. On certain occasions like special anniversaries of his or her enthronement a monarch would grant an amnesty in order to highlight the benign nature of his or her rule. Such amnesties were of an arbitrary nature. Since the beginning of World War I the use of amnesties became more pragmatic. Amnesties now came to be proclaimed also for particular political or even military ends. At the beginning of World War I an amnesty was used in Germany to make men who had been inmates of prisons available for the war effort. Meanwhile there has been a general trend to reduce the arbitrariness or discretion allowed to the representative head of a state in the granting of an amnesty. In general amnesties are now being proclaimed on the basis of a particular law passed by the legislature of a state. A new category of amnesties has emerged in the form of reform amnesties. Such an amnesty is used as a temporary correction for a law that has become outdated and that has not as yet been replaced by new legislation. Implicitly, the granting of such an amnesty suggests the obligation of the legislator to follow up the amnesty by a new law so as to make the granting of further amnesties for the offence or alleged offence that is at stake superfluous. In spite of the trend towards a degree of control of amnesties by the legislatures of states many experts are of the opinion that the representative head of a state should still have the power to indemnify an individual offender by an act of grace in a special case for which no legislation can make adequate provision. They are of the opinion that in exceptional cases a representative of the state who can act independently from the legislature and the judiciary has to have the power to take a final decision. Though an act of grace rests on a discretionary decision of the representative head of the state, it is expected that he or she will feel morally bound by human rights considerations.

In a situation of transition from an illegitimate dictatorial

regime to a democracy the amnesty issue presents special difficulties to a new government that has come to power in a new
constitutional dispensation. The term transition suggests that a
negotiated settlement has been reached between the contending
parties about a transfer of power according to democratic
principles and procedures. On the one hand the respect for the
principles of justice and human rights and for the victims of
oppression during the previous regime demands that offences
committed by that regime are not overlooked. The new
government acceding to power faces the task of co-operating
with the very same people whom they hold directly or indirectly
responsible for the crimes of the past. In such a situation it is
nearly inevitable that the commitment to ethical principles is
modified by political considerations.

It is suggested that under such circumstances the granting of
an amnesty should be guided by the following considerations:

1. That the experiences of other states which have recently also
    undergone a period of transition from authoritarian rule to
    democracy with regard to the amnesty issue be taken ac-count
    of (e.g. Chile, Uruguay, Argentina, Eastern Germany);
2. That no amnesty should be granted without the acknowl-
    edgement of the truth by the offender;
3. That more emphasis is placed on the disclosure of politically
    motivated offences and on acknowledgment by the offenders
    than on punishment of the offenders and reparation to the
    victims;
4. That the victims of politically motivated offences are offi-
    cially informed about the findings of the Truth and Recon-
    ciliation Commission;
5. That perpetrators of politically motivated offences be
    encouraged voluntarily to report on their involvement in
    the maintenance of an illegitimate and racist regime;
6. That the prosecution of offences should be limited to the
    most serious human rights violations such as hit squads,
    third-force activities, torture, etc., whereas the scope of
    disclosures should be far wider;
7. That punishment should be meted out only in the case of the
    most serious human rights violations, such as the killing of
    people, torture, hit squad and third-force activities, etc.;

8. That in the meting out of punishments responsibility should be accorded primarily to those who gave instructions for the offence, though the people who carried out the instructions also have to be held responsible;
9. That an offence committed in the struggle against an illegitimate regime cannot be judged on the same level as an offence committed by the defenders of that regime who held all the instruments of power and control in their hands;
10. That the time set aside for the disclosure of politically motivated crimes be limited to a defined period, so as to allow the communities to build up relationships of mutual trust again;
11. That compensation be envisaged to the victims of politically motivated offences as far as such compensation contributes towards reconciliation.

Contributions towards a Process of Healing of Wounds
An amnesty for politically motivated offences aims primarily at relieving the burden which offences of the past leave behind for the individual offenders as well as for the victims. It is, however, necessary to bear in mind that the society which has shaped the mind and the attitudes of the offender shares in the responsibility for politically motivated crimes. An amnesty should therefore be supplemented by other measures which can contribute towards the healing of wounds in society. Not only the state, but a variety of institutions of civil society could co-operate in such tasks. Examples are the following:

1. Historical research and history teaching in schools and at universities: Efforts are necessary to make the public aware which attitudes and prejudices and fears prevailing in society have contributed to an offence against humanity and resulted in the most hideous crimes, etc.
2. Steps should be considered as to how the one-sided or distorted interpretation of the nation's history through particular monuments can be rectified by reminding the public of the history of the victims of nationalism and of the sacrifices of the resistance against it. New monuments may be necessary. Exhibitions reminding people of particular events can be necessary (e.g. removals, etc.). Public debates on the interpretation of such events can be of great value.

3. Efforts are required to counteract the widely accepted view in South African society that punishment should be used by the state as a means of retribution and not as a means of contributing towards the healing and reintegration of the offender into society and towards the healing of society itself.

4. Churches have a special responsibility to examine whether their teaching and proclamation on repentance, sin, guilt, punishment, forgiveness and reconciliation makes the concern of God for reconciliation and for the recovery of humankind from the forces of destruction through Christ transparent or whether certain interpretations of biblical texts encourage hatred and violence in society. Other religious communities face similar tasks. Interfaith dialogue on issues of reconciliation and the healing of the wounds in society is of vital importance.

5. Churches and their members should highlight the strong emphasis on economic justice and sharing of resources as an integral dimension of the biblical understanding of reconciliation which commits them to be involved in the struggle for economic justice and in ventures in church and society which promote a more just distribution of resources.

6. Churches should devote great care towards facilitating opportunities for encounter and fellowship between the perpetrators and the victims of oppression during the apartheid regime and assist them to exchange their stories and experiences and fears with the view to a process of mutual acceptance and forgiveness.

7. Churches should encourage the potential of African communities for co-operative and inclusive decision-making processes and conflict resolution methods as a counterbalance to the competition between rival political parties inherent in the Western democratic tradition.

BIBLIOGRAPHY

Georgi, D. 1994. *Der Armen zu gedenken. Die Geschichte der Kollekte des Paulus für Jerusalem.* Neukirchner Verlag. 2., durchgesehene und erweiterte Auflage 1994

Taubes, J. 1993. Die politische Theologie des Paules. München: Wilhelm Fink Verlag

ACKNOWLEDGEMENTS

This chapter is an edited version of a more comprehensive article published by EFSA: edited and reprinted with their kind consent.

Dirkie Smit

Confession-Guilt-Truth-and-Forgiveness in the Christian Tradition

The editors invited me to make introductory remarks on the nature and the role of truth and reconciliation, and on guilt and forgiveness, specifically in the Christian tradition. Other contributors will have more to say about these themes in other religious traditions and world views, as well as in public life, and about the South African society and the Truth and Reconciliation Commission's work.

Now everyone knows that the Christian church has been concerned with truth and reconciliation, with confession, guilt and forgiveness, from its beginnings. That is what the Christian gospel is all about. In order to remind ourselves of the nature and role of these themes in Christianity, I recall a few important connections within Christian faith in which these issues find their proper place, namely the connections between *memory and confession*, between *confession and guilt*, between *guilt and truth*, and between *truth and forgiveness*. I then remind us of the important role given within Christianity to confession *to one another*, to *forgiving* one another, and to *the public nature* of this confession and this forgiveness. Finally, I mention some serious *objections* often made against these ideas within the Christian tradition.

On Memory and Confession in the Christian Tradition
Christian faith is based on memory. To remember is a funda-

mental activity of Christian faith. In every worship service the Christian community remembers. We remember the good news, the gospel. We remember the story of Christ's life, suffering, death and resurrection. Christian worship is rooted in remembering. God urges us to remember, to commemorate, and the congregation is reminded and exhorted to remember, to celebrate, to be renewed and transformed, and to love God and others.

As a major part of this act of remembering, the worshipping community is also called *to confess*. We confess who we are, we confess our guilt, we agree with God's judgement, we confess our faith and trust in God's promises.

Confession literally means to acknowledge, to agree with God's judgement on your nature, your distinctive identity, your particular past, your personal deeds. For Christians, confession means no longer attempting to suppress or deny your deepest nature, but to acknowledge the rightness of God's judgement on you, to see yourself and your past as God and as your neighbours see and remember you and your past.

In the remembrance and the confession Christians experience "the liturgy of liberation". Without such remembrance and such acknowledgement or confession there can be no freedom and no reconciliation. No freedom is possible *from* the past or *for* the future. No reconciliation *with God, with ourselves, or with others* is possible.

We must remember and confess in order to be reconciled *with God*. All Christians know that. We must, however, also remember in order to be reconciled *with ourselves*, in order to be healed. Recently, Jaap Durand argued convincingly for the need to remember in order not to lose our identity. In an essay called "In conscious remembrance" (*In bewuste herinnering*), he claims that "a successful attempt to forget will mean a complete loss of identity, individually as well as collectively". We cannot flee forever, in fear for our own pasts, trying to forget, suppressing our memories and denying our identities.

We must also remember in order to be reconciled *with one another*. In fact, in the Christian tradition remembering becomes a fundamental form of loving God and one another. The authoritative ecumenical theologian, Dietrich Ritschl, says somewhere that this is the most fundamental test of our mutual love: "*We love only those with whom we are prepared to share our story and in whose story we want to have a share. Only those who share memories and hopes really belong together.*"*

Or, in the words of one of most famous twentieth-century North American theologians, H. Richard Niebuhr, in his epoch-making work on *The Story of Our Life*: "Where common memory is lacking, where people do not share in the same past there can be no real community, and where community is to be formed common memory must be created ... The measure of our distance from each other in our nations and our groups can be taken by noting the divergence, the separateness and lack of sympathy in our social memories. Conversely the measure of our unity is the extent of our common memory."

On Confession and Guilt in the Christian Tradition
Yet it is equally clear in the Christian tradition that this remembrance, this remembering, is not a simple matter at all. An integral part of our pasts, our stories, our identities, are *the stories of pain inflicted on one another and therefore the stories of our guilt*. Richard Niebuhr discusses this crucial insight of the Christian tradition in a striking way. It may be helpful to reflect on some of his comments. He argues that *we do not really know what we have done – and are still doing – to one another. We have no idea of the effect of our actions on others, not even on those who are the closest to us.*

Niebuhr then claims that the Christian revelation helps Christians to interpret *the past*, *the present* and *the future*. Without revelation, we interpret all three of these in terms of "the evil images in out hearts". Without the light of revelation, we like to believe that everything revolves around us. We reconstruct the past around ourselves, we see the present in terms of our own interests, and we hope for a future centred around ourselves. The light of revelation, however, enables us to break through these "evil interpretations" of the past, the present, and the future.

How can that happen? With respect to the *past* revelation helps Christians in three ways, according to Niebuhr. Firstly, *it makes the past comprehensible*. He explains: "In the presence of

---

*Italics in quotations from other authors are mine.

(Christ) the Christian church can and must remember ... the long story of ... brutality and sin, the nameless sufferings of untold generations, the groaning and travailing of creation until now – all that otherwise is remembered only with despair. There is no part of the past that can be ignored."

Secondly, *the revelation in Christ urges us to remember what we have forgotten*. He says: "By reasoning on the basis of revelation the heart not only understands what it remembers but is enabled and driven to remember what it had forgotten. When we use insufficient and evil images of the personal or social self we drop out of our consciousness or suppress those memories which do not fit in with the picture we cherish. We bury our follies and our transgressions of our own law, our departures from our own ideal, in the depths of our unconsciousness. We also forget much of what seems to us trivial ... We do not destroy this past of ours; it is indestructible. We carry it with us; its record is written deep into our lives. We only refuse to acknowledge it as our true past and try to make it an alien thing – something that did not happen to our real selves. So our national histories do not recall to the consciousness of citizens the crimes and absurdities of past social conduct, as our written and unwritten biographies fail to mention our shame. But this unremembered past endures ... Our buried past is mighty; the ghosts of our fathers and of the selves that we have been haunt our days and nights though we refuse to acknowledge their presence."

Thirdly, *it helps us also to make the past of others our own*. In his words: "When people enter into a new community they not only share the present life of their new companions but also adopt as their own the past history of their fellows ... *'Where common memory is lacking, where people do not share in the same past there can be no real community, and where community is to be formed common memory must be created'*; hence the insistence on the teaching of history in modern national communities. By the aid of such provincial memories only partial pasts can be appropriated and only limited human communities can be formed."

At the same time, he argues, all of this makes *confession of guilt* so essential. Christ "resurrects this buried past (and) demands and permits that we bring into the light of attention our betrayals and denials, our follies and sins. There is nothing

99

in our lives, in our autobiographies and our social histories, that does not fit in. In the personal inner life revelation requires the heart to recall the sins of the self and to confess fully what it shuddered to remember ... And every social history, not least that of the church itself, when recollected in the light of revelation, becomes a confession of sin." For Christians this kind of remembering is consequently "a moral event", "*a conversion of the memory*". "Through Jesus Christ Christians can and must turn again and again to history, making the sins and the faiths of their fathers and brothers their own faiths and sins," he says. This "conversion of the memory", which alone can make genuine solidarity possible, is never completed, but remains "a permanent revolutionary moment". It must go on throughout the whole of a lifetime because the past is infinite and because sin enters anew in repeated efforts to separate ourselves from God and our fellow human beings through the separation of our past from them. "*The conversion of the past must be continuous because the problems of reconciliation arise in every present ... Groups use their separate histories as means of defending themselves against the criticism of others and weapons for warfare upon rival parties. We cannot become integrated parts ... until we each remember our whole past, with its sins, through Jesus Christ and appropriate each other's pasts.*"

As far as *the present* is concerned, he argues that *we do not know what we are doing to others*: "We do not know what we are doing by our aggressions and participations, our inactions and isolations from conflict ... In our smaller communities, in our families and with our friends the same ignorance is our portion. We do not know as parents, save in fragmentary ways, what we are doing to our children. We do not understand what our most intimate friends, our husbands and wives are doing to us and neither do they know."

Niebuhr concludes that in all attempts at reconciliation the following needs to be borne in mind: "No mere desire to overcome differences of opinion is of any avail unless it expresses itself in such reinterpretation and appropriation of what lies back of opinion – the memory ... *The measure of our distance from each other in our nations and groups can be taken by noting the divergence, the separateness and lack of sympathy in our social memories. Conversely the measure of our unity is the extent of our common memory* ... Our human history cannot be reconstructed save with the aid of repentance and faith; none of the national images people employ in interpreting and recalling their past suffice to bring unity."

On Guilt and Truth in the Christian Tradition

We are not reconciled with one another, claims the Christian tradition, because we do not truly understand who we are and what we are doing to one another. Precisely because we do not know who we are and what we have done and are doing, *the truth about us must be told to us*. It must come from the outside, from others, from God and from other human beings. We need others to remind us of the truth about ourselves.

The "truth" which is at stake in this common remembrance, in these mutually told stories, is thus also no simple matter. The Christian church and theology have always been interested in this question of truth. Pilate's famous question in fact is a kind of concise statement of the complex search for truth in the Christian tradition. For Christians, the truth involves more than mere information, more than precision, more than brute fact. It is also personal, human, subjective, perspective-bound, narrative, dialogic, social. The truth is always more than our truth, more than we currently know or see. We need others in order to hear their experience of the truth and attempt to make this our own.

The well-known Black theologian, James Cone, therefore claims that telling one another about memories, stories and experiences is the only way to truth, the only way in which ideological gulfs between people, groups and communities may be bridged and done away with. "Indeed, when I understand truth as story, I am more likely to be open to other people's truth stories. As I listen to other stories, I am invited to move out of the subjectivity of my own story into another realm of thinking and acting. The same is true for others when I tell my story ... Indeed, it is only when we refuse to listen to another story that our own story becomes ideological, that is, a closed system incapable of hearing the truth."

This makes confession possible. Confession, to Christians, means listening to these stories, to the story of God and to the stories of others, and recognising ourselves and our own identities and actions in these stories, and agreeing with them, acknowledging them, confessing them, accepting this about ourselves, calling ourselves by the names God and others call us.

Precisely for this reason the famous twentieth-century Protestant theologian, Karl Barth, referred to the Christian confession of guilt as *an exercise in name-giving*.

In one of the best theological works on the function and nature of the confession of guilt in the Christian church – a work dedicated to Helen and Theo Kotzé of the Christian Institute – Theodore Jennings explains: "*The corporate practice of confession teaches us to see*. It teaches us to see ourselves in the light of God's action and promise. The practice of confession is practice in the banishment of illusion, of self-deception, of dishonesty. *It is practice in honesty, in telling the truth*. The words we use here in public serve as a barrier against the practice of deceit, hypocrisy, and self-deception by which we hide ourselves from God, from our neighbour, from ourselves. ... Together and aloud we confess our sins by name. These are *our* sins we confess. We are not here describing someone else. We sometimes encounter the temptation to confess someone else's sin – to deflect attention away from ourselves. We must take care not to do this. ... In the act of confession, we become those who "see clearly" both ourselves and the world in which we are implicated. ... *The confession of sins is the point at which we ... describe ourselves as those who were blind but are now beginning to see ... In this seeing we also engage in naming ... So long as we use the wrong name for things, we cannot hope for freedom ... Names have power. They have the power to hold in bondage, to destroy and maim ... With the wrong names we can't deal appropriately with ourselves or with one another ... Confession is practice in naming ...*"

In order to be able to give a name, to be in agreement, to concur, and to admit that the other is right, those parts of the past of which you are unaware – for whatever reason – must also be made known to you by the other, from the outside. This happens in various ways in the Christian worship service. It also happens in everyday Christian life in our engagement with others and in listening to their experiences from their perspectives.

On Truth and Forgiveness in the Christian Tradition

But is this truth about ourselves not unbearable? Is it not impossible to listen to what God and others say about us and to agree with their claims? According to the Christian gospel it only becomes possible for this truth – about who we really are, about our pasts, about the suffering we have inflicted upon others and the guilt we have brought upon ourselves – not to become unbearable, not in fact to become something that we must push aside, repress, avoid or deny, when we acknowledge *the more comprehensive truth of the love, mercy, forgiveness and acceptance of God.* This is the heart of the Christian Gospel. God reconciled the world with Godself in Christ. God took mercy on the godless, the unjust, the guilty, in fact, on God's enemies. And the Christian church has been given this message of reconciliation to proclaim and administer.

It is because Christians believe this that they do not have to flee – not from God, not from their neighbours or fellow human beings, not from their own identities or from their own conscious or unconscious past. It is because Christians believe this that they can listen to the stories about themselves as told to them by others. It is because Christians believe this that they can acknowledge and confess their guilt freely, that they can progress to concrete naming instead of denial and escape.

First forgiveness, then acknowledgement of guilt. This conviction is deeply rooted in the Calvinist tradition in particular: true self-knowledge, true consciousness of sin, true acknowledgement of guilt are the consequences, the fruit, of forgiveness and not the condition leading to forgiveness. It is not the law, accusations, and threats of judgement, but Christ's cross and his atoning death that lead to mortification, contrition and repentance on the part of Christians. Jennings therefore correctly discusses confession of guilt as a facet, a component, of *The liturgy of liberation.* He paraphrases Karl Barth as follows: "The only sin we know is sin that has already been forgiven. We do not see the problem until we have been grasped by the solution." The well-known parable of the forgiven (but unforgiving!) man in Matthew 18 powerfully demonstrates this important connection.

Ten years ago – during what were still the crisis years of the struggle – Jaap Durand could therefore say: Christians know that they have been forgiven and this knowledge and assurance liberate them to act in the present. No matter how unique and distinctive the past of each Christian believer is, there is a common feature in Christians' experience of their past, something that is not shared by non-Christians. This experience is the realisation of forgiveness, very specifically the forgiveness on the cross of Jesus Christ. For Christians their past stands in the sign of the cross. In the knowledge that they have been crucified with Christ (Rom 6:6) they accept that the old things have passed away (2 Cor 5:17). This experience of the past leaves its mark in a decisive way on their experience of the present. They know that they have been forgiven and this frees them to act in the present. There is nothing which can so paralyse people in the present as a past in which they have not been purified and which leaves the question of guilt unresolved ... Through faith Christians draw the past of the cross of Christ and thereby forgiveness too towards them in the present moment so that their decisions and actions in the present also take place in forgiveness."

On the basis of this he then argued that the decisions and deeds of Christians in the present are determined "by the forgiveness from whence they come and the love towards which they proceed". In the last part of the paper he spoke explicitly about "the unresolved question of guilt" in South Africa: "From the Christian experience of time they can profess with great conviction to everyone that *people lose their freedom to act significantly in the present if they have not been cleansed in the past and the question of guilt remains unresolved ... Guilt cannot disappear by itself. The recognition and the acknowledgement of guilt form an essential link in the chain of the dissolution of guilt. Without such recognition and acknowledgement the guilt hangs like an albatross round your neck and binds you to a past which does not stand in the sign of forgiveness ... The issue of the guilt of the past and the present is, as far as I am concerned, the most important question that can be raised with regard to the South African situation ...* South Africa has a past which hangs like an albatross around its neck. We all bear the burden of that albatross, individually and collectively, Christian and non-Christian alike. But Christians have the greater responsibility in this regard because they know better than others that a past which has not been purified removes from the present the possibility of freely acting in new and innovative ways" (free translation).

In the Christian tradition, forgiveness frees us to confess. Reconciliation evokes shame and contrition. This undeserved love drives us to repentance and a change of heart.

On Confession *To One Another* in the Christian Tradition

This forgiveness, this reconciliation, this undeserved love also makes it possible – and necessary – to confess our guilt *to one another*. This is a key idea in the Christian tradition. In Luther's famous words: "A strange confessor! His name is one another!" The guilt is not only confessed to God in the private sphere. The guilt spoken about in the Old and the New Testaments almost always has a social dimension. We commit an offence against God because we commit offences against one another. We desecrate the Name of God because we violate and insult those made in God's image. We serve or spurn Christ in the way we live with those closest to us. We afflict God's Holy Spirit in our failed social relations. *If we wish to confess this guilt to God, then we are sent to confess it to one another.*

The Bible often makes this point. *Christian faith without reconciliation with those aggrieved people amongst our fellow humans is impossible.* This point is for example made strikingly clear in the Book of James. Here we are warned against conflict and division in the congregations. They are not whole and integrated, "perfect" and "healthy". They vilify one another. The rich wrong the poor. A kind of class conflict emerges. Those who are privileged are judged most severely. Ultimately the faithful must confess their guilt to one another. Then they are healed jointly – and made whole and perfect.

The Christian tradition is deeply imbued with the notion that *guilt leaves no one whole, unviolated,* unpolluted, as it were. This emerges, for example, in the Christian doctrine of original sin: everyone, from infancy, is drawn into a network of flawed relationships, mutual suffering and common guilt. No one is above this. No one lives a pure and holy life, with clean hands. In our reactions to the guilt of others we too become guilty through what we do or do not do, say or do not say, neglect or do not neglect. Obviously there are differences of degree. Naturally some do one thing and others do another. But no one is simply good or simply bad. When individuals or groups are demonised, or persecuted as witches, or driven out or stoned as scapegoats, then some of the most basic convictions of the Christian tradition are belied.

This may be seen, for example, in the Christian conviction that there is no neutral, innocent or, as it were, objective position from which people can speak of sin and guilt as impartial observers. These things cannot be investigated, studied and analysed, explained and clarified, and commented on from an external perspective. The point is often made in the tradition that the only Christian way to talk about guilt is to confess it.

This becomes clear, for example, in the Christian conviction that guilt is not primarily located in what we do or have done, not in isolated deeds, but in the person himself or herself, in our nature, our being, our identity. We cannot separate ourselves from our actions and think that we have in fact done something wrong, or that we have failed in some respect, but that on the whole we are not doing too badly. In terms of the classic Christian tradition such a moralistic, legalistic, action-orientated view of sin and guilt is extremely superficial. The most profound spiritual problem is not what and how we are doing, but *who we really are*.

In Christian liberation theology, for example, these kinds of convictions (implication in the web of original sin and guilt; no objective, innocent position outside of sin; not only single, isolated deeds) are often expressed in convictions related to the structural and systemic nature of sin and guilt.

In short, it is therefore always extremely difficult and highly problematic in the Christian church to speak of "their" guilt, as if some are guilty and others not. Church leaders and theologians have often attempted to do this but it remains a suspect undertaking. It is much more typical of the Christian tradition rather to speak – whenever distinctions are made – of "*us*" rather to see, recognise and confess the communality of guilt, to take upon oneself willingly the shared quality of guilt and in this way bear the burden of the other according to the law and example of Christ, the Innocent who suffered for the guilty. In the Christian tradition confession is not an exercise in pointing out guilt and in self-justification, but in *communal adoption and acceptance of the shared guilt*.

106

Very instructive, in this regard, are the insights and convictions of the martyred minister and theologian in Nazi Germany, Dietrich Bonhoeffer. Throughout his life personal, mutual confession, the "confession of sins to one another" remained of the utmost importance for Bonhoeffer. Thus, in his famous little book called *Life Together*, in which he explains life in the underground training seminar of the Confessing Church at Finkenwalde, he uses James 5:16 as his point of departure in dealing with the need for confession in the community of the faithful: " 'Confess your sins to each other (James 5:16). He who is alone with his sin is utterly alone. It may be that Christians, notwithstanding corporate worship, common prayer, and all their fellowship in service, may still be left to their loneliness. The final breakthrough to fellowship does not occur, because ... they do not have fellowship as sinners. The pious fellowship permits no one to be a sinner. So everybody must conceal his sin from himself and from the fellowship. We dare not be sinners." But mercifully God confronts us with the truth that we are sinners and yet still accepts us. We no longer have to live the lie. This blessing – being able to confess – has been granted to the church in the brothers and sisters who take Christ's place and to whom we can confess so that they may absolve us.

Even more important for Bonhoeffer was the fact that this opens the way to *community*. "Sin demands to have man by himself. The more isolated a man is, the more destructive will be the power of sin over him, and the more deeply he becomes involved in it, the more disastrous is his isolation. Sin wants to remain unknown. ... The sin must be brought to light. The unexpressed must be openly spoken and acknowledged. All that is secret and hidden is made manifest. It is a hard struggle until the sin is openly admitted. But God breaks gates of brass and iron."

The paradox is precisely that Bonhoeffer, who was not, one could say, quite so directly implicated in the guilt, campaigned so strongly for confession and preceded the church in confessing. And as it became increasingly clear that the vast majority of Germans did not share this contrition and confession, he resorted increasingly to vicarious confession and vicarious actions, including adoption of guilt. In fact, when Bonhoeffer became involved in the resistance in order to put a spoke in the wheels and try to prevent Hitler's regime from committing further injustice and inflicting further misery, he was fully aware as a Christian believer that he was committing a "sin", becoming "guilty", doing what is wrong, for which he would have to be forgiven. He knew that the guilt of the other could not justify his own resistance and conspiracy. *He knew that he was being drawn into a web of guilt, that he could not claim that their evil justified what he was doing.* According to Christian belief, one cannot put right one wrong by committing a second wrong. He also prayed for forgiveness for what he felt he had to do, and put his trust in God's mercy rather than in his own merits.

And after the World War the same adoption of guilt in solidarity happened again in the much publicised and famous Stuttgart Confession of the German Evangelical Church. There again it was those whom one would have thought were not so guilty, or at least less guilty, who vicariously took the guilt upon themselves on behalf of the others. They charged themselves with "not confessing even more courageously, not praying more faithfully, not believing with greater joy, and not loving more fervently". Those people whom one could say were more directly implicated in the guilt, in human terms, rejected the confession, asked contemptuously who gave the others the right or the mandate to confess in that way, and wanted to know whether they were an official delegation with the right to speak in that way.

On *Forgiving* One Another in the Christian Tradition

Yet Christian life is not only an exercise in the confession of guilt. It is also, and in fact in the first place, *the practice of forgiveness.* The readiness and the ability to forgive is a primary Christian virtue. If the Christian community is "a community of character", as many people would like to call it, a community in which people with a certain kind of character, vision, virtue and values are cultivated and formed, then the virtue of being able to forgive must surely be one of their most important character-istics. The church must be *Embodying Forgiveness*, the title of a recent study by Gregory Jones. He characterises the Christian God as the Triune God who forgives and who, through the Spirit, transforms a community to become "a trinitarian community ... practising forgiveness".

There can be no doubt about this. *A culture of mutual*

forgiveness should prevail in a Christian community. The reason for this is obvious. The logic, the grammar, of this Christian culture of forgiveness is very closely linked to the logic and grammar of the Christian gospel itself. Christians forgive because they have been forgiven. Christians embrace others as they have been embraced by Christ. In technical theological language: the imperative is rooted in the indicative. Biblical documents and the Christian tradition are full of this logic. One of the best known examples is the parable in Chapter 18 of the Gospel of Matthew about the debtor who was let off his debts but who on the steps of the palace already failed to show the same disposition.

It is important to understand this, because there are also many other sound arguments for forgiving others. One of the most famous examples is the highly popular work of the North American evangelical theologian and writer, Lewis Smedes, whose book is entitled *Forgive and Forget.* According to Smedes one must forgive *for one's own sake, for the sake of one's own spiritual health and one's own future.* No matter how important such arguments are, their logic, their grammar, still differs from the language of Christian forgiveness. Perhaps it may be helpful to consider this in some detail.

Smedes is interested in healing people who have suffered pain at some time in their past which still damages and destroys their lives in the present. "Some old pains ... remain like stubborn stains in the fabric of our own memory. Deep hurts we never deserved flow from our dead past into our living present."

He thinks that what is necessary is what Hannah Arendt (in her very famous study on *The Human Condition*) called "The faculty of forgiveness ... the only power that can stop the inexorable stream of painful memories". Smedes writes that forgiveness of undeserved pain is a process consisting of four stages: "we hurt; we hate; we heal ourselves; we come together".

Sometimes the fourth stage, the climax that occurs when true reconciliation is achieved between people, never takes place. Yet, he says, it is so important for the person who has experienced unjustified suffering that the third stage should occur, that is, that people will be healed inwardly so that they can live without the self-destructive pain and hatred, that this in itself makes forgiveness absolutely essential.

He is concerned only with *personal pain* ("We can only forgive people, we cannot forgive nature ... Nor can we forgive systems ... People are the only ones that can be held accountable for what they do. People are the only ones who can accept forgiveness and decide to come back to us"), *unjustified* pain and *deeply rooted* pain. When he describes the stages he explicitly points out that forgiveness is not to be equated with some of the other things with which it is often confused: "Forgiving is not forgetting; Excusing is not forgiving; Forgiving is not the same as smothering conflict; Accepting people is not forgiving them; Forgiving is not tolerance."

In an important chapter he deals with the fact that there are people who find it extremely difficult to forgive and in fact for whom it may be impossible to forgive. Particularly difficult is "Forgiving the invisible people" (the invisible, anonymous people, who are collectively guilty, but who are unknown and impersonal); "Forgiving people who do not care; and: Forgiving monsters".

He finally considers the question as to *why* one should forgive, why this is, as it were, better than not to forgive. For him the primary reason is the happiness and health of those who do the forgiving, "our need to forgive *for our own sakes* ... Every human soul has a right to be free from hate, and we claim our rightful inheritance when we forgive people who hurt us unfairly."

This is why the third stage – "We heal ourselves" – is so important for him: "Pull your mind away from the person who needs to be forgiven; do not ask yet what happens to the forgiven wrongdoer. *Look only at the wounded forgiver* ... When you forgive someone for hurting you, you perform spiritual surgery inside your soul ... You may be the only person healed ... [The other person] is out of your control ... So when you forgive you must often be content with the editing of your own memory. *It is the editing of your memory that is your salvation ... If you cannot ... you enslave yourself to your own painful past, and by fastening yourself to the past, you let your hate become your future. You can reverse your future only by releasing other people from their pasts.*"

This is why, he says, we must also forgive those who are unrepentant. "So we need to forgive the unrepentant *for our own sake*. We need to forgive people who do not care if only so that

110

we do not drown in our own misery. Let the other guy take care of himself."

It is particularly with respect to the latter point that Smedes has been sharply criticised. Roberts, for example, writes: "Smedes offers a particular conception of forgiveness ... one ... interestingly different from and at odds with that of classical Christianity ... The kind of forgiveness that Smedes expounds both overlaps with Christian forgiveness and is significantly different from it." In what way does Smedes's "therapeutic" forgiveness differ from that of "Christian" forgiveness? Roberts notes a range of differences but the most important is that the motive in Smedes is "healing of the self". This is by no means absent from Christian forgiveness, but it does not form the paradigm of forgiveness. "When asked for a rationale for forgiveness, Paul does not speak in therapeutic terms, but in terms of what is fitting, given certain beliefs about the history of God's actions, the character and actions of Jesus, the nature of the church and the coming kingdom."

To put this in a different way: *according to the Christian paradigm we do not forgive because we want to heal ourselves, but because we have been forgiven.* Roberts notes that the spirit of the times, the *spirituality of the culture* (in Western countries), as it were, is not very receptive these days to this Christian kind of call for forgiveness. "In an age when people are focused on their own physical fitness and psychological well-being as the noblest and most basic motives for every action, the Pauline rationale for forgiveness will be far less persuasive than the therapeutic one."

On *Public* Confession and Forgiveness in the Christian Tradition
Do we, however, also have to confess to one another *in public*? And do we have to forgive one another and receive forgiveness *in public*? It is clear from what has already been said why confession and contrition in the Christian faith have *both a* cultic, liturgical, official, *public* and collective form *as well as a personal*, voluntary, private, subjective and spontaneous *form* – and why there is *a constant tension* between these two forms.

In the former – the communal confession of guilt in the Christian liturgy – the vicarious dimension comes to the fore more strongly. In this case the faithful take the guilt upon themselves for sins in which they were not directly implicated. Here they learn to say "we" and receive common, official and public absolution. They also celebrate this forgiveness. As a liturgical moment, a symbolic act, a voluntary adoption of guilt, it is of fundamental importance.

Yet it is not sufficient. It can too easily become meaningless, simply objective, simply cultic, simply official, merely ritual, without any subjective identification, without genuine contrition, without true introspection and a change of heart among individual believers.

This is why the second form is also necessary: personal, interpersonal confession, in marriages and families, in relations with friends, in all kinds of mutual ways of living together. In this way, too, Christians need to practise confession, personally, by name, with contrition, and with introspection and a change of heart.

Many practices have developed in the various Christian traditions as attempts to institutionalise this essential aspect of Christian life. During the times of the early church problems had already arisen with regard to those who sinned after they became Christians. By the Third Century a system of public confession, contrition and repentance had already developed. It was regarded as a kind of second baptism and it was extremely strict in the requirements set for prayers, fasting and alms. At one stage sinners even had to join confessional orders and were prohibited from doing certain things, such as getting married, for the rest of their lives. From the sixth century Celtic and Anglo-Saxon missionaries began increasingly to establish practices of repeated, private confession before a priest on the European mainland. During the Fourth Lateran Council (1215) private confession became officially established. Every Christian had to confess his or her sins at least once a year. By this time the prayer of the priest for the sinner – compare James's "pray for one another" – had changed into the granting of absolution or forgiveness itself. In time more and more practices developed around confession. The revised *Ordo Poenitentiae* (1973) of the Catholic Church contains three different rites for reconciliation. In general the emphasis in Catholic Christianity now falls on a more pastoral understanding of the sacrament, with more attention to the corporate nature of sin and reconciliation as well as to the working of the Holy Spirit in the renewal of life.

The resistance in the Reformation was largely against the increasingly comprehensive intermediary role which the ecclesiastical hierarchy began to play in confession and forgiveness, with the many accompanying practices; a plea was made in the Reformation for the restoration of the direct relationship between the faithful and God in contrition, confession and receiving merciful forgiveness. Luther's famous theses called for continuous and public confession and renewal. Reconciliation, according to the Christian tradition, "must become real in history" (Jonker), it must become effective and visible in our daily lives with others. It is not enough to confess privately, individually, before God, alone, without anyone knowing.

When Christians truly practice these convictions in public, their "forgiveness in politics" becomes an extraordinary *ethic for enemies*, as the well-known theologian Donald Shriver Jr. argues in a recent study.

On Objections to Confession-Guilt-Truth-and-Forgiveness in the Christian Tradition

In conclusion: obviously not everyone, either within or outside the Christian community, thinks that the conjunction of confession-guilt-truth-and-forgiveness in the Christian tradition is a good thing. Let us remind ourselves of *four important forms of criticism*.

In the *first* place, there are people who consider this a sign of spiritual illness. One of the recent classic critical discussions of this "morbid" mentality, this erroneous concentration on and attempt to evoke "false guilt feelings" within Christian piety is that of the authoritative Lutheran theologian, Wolfhart Pannenberg. In an essay on "Protestant piety and guilt consciousness" in his study on Christian spirituality, Pannenberg is sharply critical of the dominating role of guilt and feelings of guilt in Protestant, and more specifically Lutheran, spirituality. He identifies himself with what he describes as an actual loss of guilt feelings in Protestant circles, "the critical dissolution of guilt consciousness". He sees this loss of guilt feelings not as a weakness or a danger, because they should in any event never have been so prevalent. He interprets the emphasis on guilt feelings and the need to confess guilt as a wrongful development in Christendom. According to him it is no surprise that it was in the sphere of Protestantism that a very powerful reaction to this mentality arose. He discusses the criticism of Nietzsche (especially in his famous *Genealogy of Morals*, 1887) and Freud (especially in his *Totem and Taboo*, 1913) of the mentality of guilt feelings and says that to this day these views have not yet been taken sufficiently seriously in the Christian churches. The core of his critique is in fact that guilt feelings and the confessional mentality, which have become the root of the experience of God in Protestantism, are unmasked as a spiritual illness, as pathological and neurotic. Nietzsche reacted strongly to the atmosphere of "cultivation of guilt feelings" in which he was raised. He rebelled against this moralistic attitude and self-hatred of the pietist disposition and postulated a new "self-sufficient innocence" in opposition to it. "He diagnosed bad conscience as a mental disease, a case of interiorised aggression". According to Nietzsche this was the most catastrophic development of all in the history of European thinking. Freud proffered similar ideas, extended to religion as phenomenon – according to him "a mass neurosis arising from guilt consciousness".

Secondly, there are people who warn that society is not the church. Its citizens are not identical with the Christian believers. South Africa is not the kingdom of God. We do not have a theocratic form of government. The logic of Christian confession of guilt and forgiveness is not the logic of the public, political and economic world. The grammar of Christian contrition, confession and absolution is not the grammar of public jurisprudence. In the public sphere Smedes's logic probably makes more sense than that of Matthew 18. Religious forgiveness is not amnesty.

Here we confront the complex questions of Christian social ethics, of the relationship between the church, state and society, of the public church and civil society. This is not the place to discuss the many permutations of the answers to these difficult questions. Other contributions will do that. It is sufficient to remember that there are no direct links between Christian convictions and behaviour and public life in a modern democracy. We have already taken long enough to learn this.

Thirdly, there are those who warn that the Christian church(es) should not be too quick and too eager to speak about guilt, particularly if we are thinking about the guilt of others. The Christian tradition has enough guilt of its own, they say. In many ways we must first learn to confess ourselves; we must ourselves still discover the truth about ourselves, they claim. Again, there is an important element of truth in this accusation.

Fourthly, there are those who argue that "the search for the truth" and "confessions of guilt" can easily become ideologised, that they too can simply become weapons in a social power struggle. This would amount to cynically using processes which should and could be healing for societies as instruments in continuing power struggles.

The Christian tradition should take these warnings and criticisms seriously. However, it is also possible to argue that the Christian convictions about confession-guilt-truth-and-forgiveness can still help societies in several ways.

a) Perhaps the Christian tradition could help societies with a moral interpretation of their past, with *facing up to the truth of what happened and still happens*. The church should be embodying confession and embodying forgiveness. The Christian church should not attempt to deny the truth about the past, or fear the future, or ignore the realities of the present. Christians experience the liturgy of liberation so that they can face the truth.

b) The Christian tradition could help societies to remember that *confession is not easy, that forgiveness is not cheap, that reconciliation is not superficial.* They all bear a price. They all call for courage, for commitment. They all cause pain. They all deeply affect the people involved. They all radically challenge, change and transform us. They must not be confused with the instant and cheap solutions that often masquerade for them and even carry their names.

c) The Christian tradition could perhaps also remind societies that *guilt is more pervasive than we usually think*; that the truth is more complex than we would sometimes wish; that it is indispensable that we should have a common past, a common memory, which means that we shall have to listen, and hear – repeatedly, no matter how terrible the stories of pain inflicted; that genuine contrition is born from the knowledge of genuine forgiveness.

d) The Christian tradition could perhaps also remind societies of the danger that people everywhere wish to excuse themselves for what happened in their past. This produces a destructive cycle. The *chain of denial of guilt and accusation of others is potentially endless* and – as we have often seen through the centuries – potentially devastating in the long run. The Christian tradition can perhaps recognise this process for what it is and warn against it. Seeking scapegoats ultimately leads to new, never-ending violence.

e) And perhaps the Christian tradition can remind societies that *"forgetting"* is an ambiguous matter. There is indeed *a Christian instruction not to forget*. The Christian church depends upon this, for many reasons. One is that we must remember so that we can learn from the past, so that it "will never happen again". Yet there is *also a Christian instruction to forget*. Forgetting can also be a moral activity. The wonder of the message of the gospel for Christians is precisely that God removes our sins from us as far as the east is removed from the west and never again thinks of them. It is one thing to say: we forgive, but we cannot forget. It is another to say: we forgive, but we shall never, we may never, we never wish to, we will never forget. The Christian tradition is ultimately based on the trust that God-in-Christ does not speak to the world like that, and calls us to speak and live accordingly.

BIBLIOGRAPHY
Bonhoeffer, D. 1983. *Life Together*. London: SCM
Cone, J. 1974. *God of the Oppressed*. New York: Seabury Press
Durand, J.J. 1986. *Teks binne Konteks. Versamelde Opstelle oor Kerk en Politiek*. Bellville: UWC
—— 1993. In Bewuste Herinnering. *Intellektueel in Konteks*. Pretoria: HSRC
Jennings, T. 1988. *The Liturgy of Liberation*. Nashville: Abingdon
Jones, G. 1995. *Embodying Forgiveness*. Grand Rapids: Eerdmans

Niebuhr, H. R. 1941. *The Meaning of Revelation*. New York: Macmillan

Pannenberg, W. 1984. *Christian Spirituality and Sacramental Community*. London: Dartmann, Longman and Todd

Ritschl, D. 1986. *The Logic of Theology*. London: SCM

Shriver, D. 1995. *An Ethic for Enemies*. Oxford: Oxford University Press

Cornel du Toit

Dealing with the Past

Alleged Problems with the Truth and Reconciliation Commission
The coverage by the Afrikaans press of the Truth and
Reconciliation Commission has been predominantly negative.
It is seen as a Pandora's box which will ridicule indemnity (*Die
Burger*, 17/1/95:10). The motivation for the Commission, that it
may contribute to the healing of the nation, is not generally
accepted. Its reconciliatory tenor is not believed. The Commission, it has been argued, will be like a square circle, as
theological motives of confession and forgiveness cannot be
harmonised with those of adjudication. A true spirit of
confession, which it is presupposed is the work of the Holy
Spirit, cannot artificially be forced upon someone. There are also
other voices raised in protest against the indemnity clause which
forestalls the possibility of prosecuting offenders. Dr Fumbatha
Mxenge's view is that nothing short of the prosecution and
conviction of those who killed his brother and his brother's wife
would ever satisfy his family (*City Press*, 8.1.95: 15).

The negative reaction can also be ascribed to the fact that the
whole process of dealing with the past is interpreted politically as
an act of retribution. The process will nourish bitterness, encourage hatred between races, and divide the nation, it is argued.
The press will latch onto the sensational. It will encourage
retributive actions and justify crime. It can be seen as a
continuation of the apartheid strategies of questioning to

confirm the final truth. The only difference is that the power balance has changed and that the sword is now in the other hand.

Nothing like the final truth exists, as truth is contextual, contingent and historical. It is precisely the apartheid regime's appeal to truth which made it such a dangerous ideology. In this regard Mr Willie Hofmeyr (ANC), acting chairman of the Justice Committee, said: "I don't think we should kid ourselves that we will have the whole truth at the end of the day. But we should know of it to set the past behind us" (*The Citizen*, 11.5.95: 6).

The debate has remained politically coloured as predominantly political arguments were heard in the debate, while arguments concerning religious and humane motives seemed not to be convincing. Mainline churches participate little, if at all, to motivate the theological and pastoral importance of the Commission.

The Reconstruction and Development Programme (RDP) concentrates predominantly on the material efforts of restoration. More attention should be given to the important process of spiritual reconstruction. One could expect that churches should have voiced their opinion in this regard.

What Do We Mean by Saying that We Must Deal with the Past?
It may be that the Truth and Reconciliation Commission will not be successful in significantly helping us to deal with the past. This makes the imperative to deal with the past no less relevant. The importance of dealing with the past surpasses the Truth and Reconciliation Commission.

When we speak of dealing with the past we use the word past in a *generic* sense predominantly referring to negative experiences which inflicted wounds on us, soiled our memory, negatively determined our identity and personhood – in other words dealing with the past from a situation where we suffer the consequences of our past. Dealing with the past does not necessarily mean that neat and precise ways of rectifying wrongs from the past exist or that it is simply a matter of deciding to restructure our identity, wipe our memory, and redefine our character.

Dealing with the past is an act of desperation – trying to find alibis for our predicaments, *trying to understand and explain*

119

ourselves – the feeling we have about our past. It means to dig as psychological archaeologists into the ruins of our past to reconstruct our lives and try to reinterpret the past from different sides. Especially on the level of personal suffering, continuous traumatic stress, unaddressed psychological hindrances and so on, the process can benefit many people.

Dealing with the past is a *historical act of interpretation*, whether we deal with our personal or national history. Our identity is explained sufficiently only when history is known: we are what we have become (Maier 1988: 150). But history is so final – it is written. Therefore we remember history in order to change history. What we have become should not fixate us as if we were confronted by an unchangeable fate.

Dealing with the past is therefore also an *act of restoration and reinterpretation* through which we redefine and reshape ourselves. In this sense the past concerns our *present and future*. Louw (1995: 149ff) states that past events should become signposts which on the one hand serve as warnings, but on the other are issued as dynamic guidelines which prevent future plans from becoming fixed ideas and blueprints.

In dealing with haunting influences from the past we concentrate on the effects the system of apartheid has had on individuals and communities and especially on specific incidents where people were treated inhumanly, were tortured, kidnapped, murdered and degraded. It must be borne in mind that many other influences, which can also be linked to apartheid, affected and still affect people. Molipa mentions the following: "Not only was suffering brought about by apartheid, but also by the people themselves. People who could not think deeply and properly caused suffering. If one looked behind these people's thinking and actions one could see and detect the workings of apartheid. In other words, apartheid used some of the people to bring about suffering to their own people" (Molipa 1995: 11).

One must be aware of the continuing influence of poverty, malnutrition, lack of education, family structures, and many other aspects which are taken for granted in a first-world context. Many of these influences will still be with us for many years and must actively be challenged if we are at all serious about combatting harmful influences on our people.

In dealing with the past we are trying to heal and not to

destroy and prosecute. The intention with the whole effort is to restore those values without which we do not consider a humane society possible: the value of respect for human life, freedom, dignity and rights. This implies saying "no" to abuse of power, especially by those entrusted with power.

What Does It Concern?
We are speaking of the past of all South Africans from all ethnic, cultural, religious and language groups. All South Africans made up the South African community, and all experienced apartheid, whether as its beneficiaries or its victims. We all have certain attitudes towards each other, mentalities that determine our identity and interaction with each other, views on and opinions about each other that are direct consequences of our past. Louw (1995: 151) indicates that change is an attitudinal problem. If structures are changed without people changing simultaneously, the problem of resistance will be experienced.

To change people takes time. We cannot, however, do without this process. There is more at stake than simply getting back at a few perpetrators. What is at stake is the value of human life and freedom, which concerns all of us. To heal the nation implies that the nation as a whole is affected. We must acknowledge that each one of us is part of this society and in some sense each of us is responsible for the way it looks. I dare never isolate myself from what is happening, in the hope that it will not directly affect me. This is poignantly expressed in the words of the theologian Martin Niemöller, who said after the collapse of the Third Reich that German Christians had "let God waiting years". The following statement sums up why Nazism got its way so long: "First they came for the socialists, and I did not speak out – because I was not a socialist. Then they came for the trade unionists, and I did not speak out – because I was not a trade unionist. Then they came for the Jews, and I did not speak out – because I was not a Jew. Then they came for me – and there was no one left to speak for me" (Roth 1987: 211). We are in principle denying justice to ourselves if we do not identify with those suffering under any form of injustice.

Dealing with the past concerns *those who benefited from apartheid*. We know that many white people still cannot understand that apartheid was wrong and harmful – not to mention sinful. They would agree that in some cases some injustices may have been committed, but it is balanced out by the "benefits" of apartheid which allowed, among other things, people to maintain their cultural and group identity. An ideology ingrained in the mode of thinking of people takes some time to change. To help this process as much as possible, information should be released on how individuals experienced the negative face of apartheid.

The process concerns also those *passively involved* in a system of oppression. In a sense all were locked in prison houses of colour, ethnicity and belief systems. The process of freeing ourselves from these bondages must be discussed.

Although difficult, we must try to distinguish between people who simply drifted along with the tide of history and those involved in actively, determinately, injuring others – those *actively involved*, in acts of violence. This must be done, bearing in mind the already-mentioned recognition of the responsibility of all. We must be careful, however, as has been cautioned so often, not to indulge in vendettas or Nuremberg-type trials. However, stories should be told which help all to understand.

Dealing with the past may take us a long way into the future. It takes time to heal. The Truth and Reconciliation Commission itself may not take longer than two years to complete its work, but the healing process itself may take as long as the lifespan of those who suffered.

The process concerns all parties simultaneously as we have to come to grips with the past and can only face the past by facing each other. To face the past means to face the person whom you have injured. We must stop speaking about one another and start speaking to each other by jointly discussing our experiences and feelings of hate, anger, guilt, shame, sorrow and so on. We must also and especially speak about the lack of feelings of guilt, shame and sorrow and an unwillingness to repent.

How Should We Go about It?
The whole effort of the Truth and Reconciliation Commission will be futile if solid motivation and justification is lacking. It must be emphasised that the Truth and Reconciliation Commission must be seen as only part of the process. To be able to say "never again!", there must be a general feeling of

outrage, indignation and resentment. This is not yet the case among all South Africans. To create this general feeling of outrage we need a few stories that will function as symbols with which to identify. So many of these stories exist from the Second World War, for example the *The Diary of Anne Frank*. It was not so much the Nuremberg trails which influenced world opinion concerning the atrocities of the Nazis, but the stories told by victims and those who showed compassion to the victims. The therapeutic value of storytelling is generally agreed upon. Stories give a face and a body to the victims of atrocities and will do so for victims of apartheid. This is the face of "the other" which confronts all religions and values, each one of us. The face of the other, the suffering "gaze", demands response.

The Place of Memory: How to Remember and How to Forget

My past is with me now. It is in my present as conscious and unconscious memory; it is here now as habits of behaviour, of speech and thought. My interpersonal past also is with me in all present meetings with other selves. It is there in all my love and guilt. The self doesn't leave past behind as does the moving hand of a clock – its past is inscribed into it more deeply than the past of geologic formations is crystallised in their present form (Niebuhr 1963: 93).

Wishing to forget the past

It takes courage to deal with the past, especially if my past is filled with feelings of guilt and shame or of suffering, horror, anxiety and fear. It is thus understandable that one often lacks the courage to face the past and prefers to let bygones be bygones. We do not wish to remember if it implies torturing ourselves.

Dealing with the past is, however, proof of your courage for the future. One wants to deal with the past in order to understand and change the present and so face the future.

Living only in the past

We cannot wipe out the past and start with a new slate as if nothing has happened to us. But we must also not get stuck in the past. We will always bear the scars inflicted upon us from the past but we must, as far as possible, overcome the pain from the wounds of the past. So many people will remain stuck in the past, because they never knew what happened in the past. *They have a right to know* so as to be able to free themselves from a past which captures them through uncertainty. Those who have lost a child or loved one and do not know what happened to them must get access to this information to set their minds at rest. As Sylvia Jele (*Weekend Star* 1995/2/5: 8) said: "I don't seek revenge, I just want to know why and how my son was killed."

But when legalism takes over, our brains become befuddled – we forget why we started down the road in the first place. Persons like Sylvia Jele must be guided through this process to find the truth that she as a mother is entitled to know. There is a truth that belongs to all, although it was known only to a few. It is the kind of truth that concerns our freedom. Truth that inhibits our freedom must be criticised and truth that advances freedom must be sought after.

Memory and identity
While there are so many things one would like to wipe from one's memory there are also many unpleasant things that must be remembered. Memory is a prerequisite for identity. It is not only what we remember, but also how we remember, how we interact with memory that co-determines our identity. We must excavate the past, not to our detriment, but to our benefit. For some, memory can overwhelm and depress; for others, less scared perhaps, it becomes addictive. History can neither be reduced to memory, nor can identity be specified in terms of history or memory alone (Maier 1988: 149). Identity and memory are open entities that can be coloured and interpreted in specific ways with different emphases.

Theological Guidelines in Dealing with the Past
From a Christian point of view several theological principles can be named according to which the past must be viewed. Only a few are cursorily mentioned: Human beings are responsible to God, their fellow humans and to themselves for their deeds. God's grace is no licence to sin. If we sincerely confess our sins God will forgive us and urge us to sin no more. It is expected from believers not to hate or persecute their enemies but to love them. We can leave the resonsibility of punishment to God. An

"eye-for-an-eye" attitude belongs to the old dispensation. We must love our neighbours and do to them as we would wish them to act towards us. God is the one who transforms us through the Spirit. The past can be put behind us.

The question is whether these principles will suffice to deal satisfactorily with all the expectations people have of the Commission. The ideal is often far removed from reality.

Excellent Christian principles were also adhered to by many of those who propagated apartheid. The film *Blue Velvet* portrayed the grim picture that the best of us are irresistibly drawn to the degrading, the brutal, and the violent. The message of the film is that people who will be most successful are those who can control their drives, hiding them when it's to their advantage and yet satisfying them when they can get away with it (Lee 1988. 583).

Guilt, contrition and confession
One can agree with Louw (1995: 152) that we need more than feelings of guilt concerning the injustices of apartheid to construct a new South Africa. We need a sincere understanding of guilt, that is, the responsibility to confess that apartheid was a sin because it violated the ethical issues of justice, neighbourly love, humanity and charity.

Personal guilt presupposes that one knew what was right and deliberately did the opposite. Often people carry their feeling of guilt alone. Because of the strong drive of self-protection, they dare not share their feelings of guilt. This lack of sharing may become unbearable and may manifest in aggression, intolerance and isolation. We often use collective guilt as an excuse for our personal guilt. We get away with the excuse of saying: "What could I have done to counter Nazism, apartheid, and so on?" Nobody takes responsibility for collective guilt and it is normally restricted to a few scapegoats who can be identified.

Forgiveness and tolerance
Forgiveness presupposes tolerance. You must be able to live with the person you have forgiven, that is, you must be able to tolerate him/her as fellow fallible human. Apartheid is a master symbol of intolerance. Under an apartheid system you separate yourself from those you cannot tolerate. Closed communities

125

breed closed minds. Tolerance must be cultivated and nurtured by all races and classes if we wish to overcome apartheid. An intolerant society remains an apartheid society. This implies tolerance on all levels – religious, sexual, racial, cultural.

Tolerance is very difficult to achieve when our mind-set is fixed in a fundamentalistic manner where final principles, petrified traditions and immovable opinions are held. Religions and theologies are culpable of breeding this attitude among its members. Intolerance is then regarded as a sign of a loyal, steadfast and unwavering spirit. When criticising this attitude we do not imply that one can be without principles, attitudes or a mind-set. What is criticised is an exclusive and absolute attitude of not allowing any nuance in the name of a final and last truth.

Forgiveness implies, according to Louw (1955: 153), not trying to exonerate somebody else's stake, not trying to forget the past, not only pardoning another for wrongdoings of the past, not liberating someone on parole for a probation period, but handing the guilt over to the grace of God to be set free with the knowledge that the past has been completely obliterated. We could only concur with this statement if it implies that real forgiveness between people becomes possible. Simply leaving everything to God may be interpreted as evading our own participation in the process of forgiveness. We do, however, agree that forgiveness, like grace, may not become cheap.

Going Along into the Future
The past is not necessarily that which lies behind us. Many of the deeds and attitudes distinctive of the past are still very much present. Many people have not changed at all. Crime enhances mistrust and negativity. People are still suffering. Democracy without bread, suffrage without shelter, freedom without job opportunities is not much of a consolation.

The ideal is to deal with the past satisfactorily so that the words of President Mandela may indeed be true: "Never, never again shall it be that this beautiful land will experience the oppression of one by another ... The sun shall never set on so glorious a human achievement. Let freedom reign. God bless Africa" (Mandela 1994: 747).

The Unique Role that Churches/Religious Groups Must Play

☐ The attention of churches/religious groups must be drawn to the fact that they have a unique and exclusive role to play.

☐ The urgency of their participation in the healing process must be indicated.

☐ Churches should be challenged to indicate how they intend participating in the process of healing and restoration.

☐ A practical Christianity/religion which is socially responsible and alert must be propagated.

☐ A theology that is socially concerned must be practised. Paul Tillich said that no statement is theological which does not contain, directly or indirectly, saving truth. And " 'saving Truth' means that truth which is done; saving truth is in him that does the truth" (Tillich 1948: 117, see also 114ff).

☐ The logic of domination so long operative in our society must be replaced by a logic of freedom, acceptance and equality (Watson 1994: 180-181).

☐ Programmes of action should be submitted as guidelines to congregations.

☐ Time should be allowed during church gatherings to have stories read or told and discussed.

☐ Opportunities should be allowed for discussing the nature, worth, and theological significance of confession, suffering, sacrifice, social involvement and so on.

☐ We must ubuntu-fy the church which implies that as a dialogical community we know that to talk is to love and to love is to talk (Botman 1995: 169).

BIBLIOGRAPHY

Botman, R. 1995. "Dealing with Diversity", in Buchanan & Hendricks 1995: 164-172

Buchanan, D. & Hendricks, J. (eds) 1995. *Meeting the Future: Christian Leadership in South Africa*. Pretoria: Knowledge resources

Lee, S. H. 1988. "The Essence of the Human Experience in David Lynch's *Blue Velvet*", in *The Essence of the Human Experience*.

Lee, S. (ed) 1988. *Inquiries into Values*. 569-583. Queenstown: Edwin Mellen Press

Louw, D 1995. "The Healing Power of Forgiveness", in Buchanan & Hendricks

Maier, C. S. 1988. *The Unmasterable Past*. Cambridge: Harvard University Press

Mandela, N 1994. *Long Walk to Freedom*. London: Abacus.

Molipa, T 1995. "A Community Gripped by Suffering", Buchanan & Hendricks 1995:7-16

Nicolson, R. B. 1994. "Does Jesus Save in South Africa?" In Mouton J. Lategan B (eds) *The Relevance of Theology for the 1990s*: 409-420. Pretoria: HSRC

Niebuhr, H. R. 1963. *The Responsible Self*. New York: Harper & Row

Roth, J. K. 1987. "Their Brother's Keepers? Christians, Churches, and Jews", in Rubenstein R. & Roth J K (eds) *Approaches to Auschwitz*, 199-228. London: SCM.

Tillich, P. 1948. *The Shaking of the Foundations*. New York: Charles Scribners's Sons.

Watson, J. R. 1994. *Between Auschwitz and Tradition. Postmodern Reflections on the Task of Thinking*. Amsterdam: Rodopi

CHALLENGE TO THE CHURCHES

Charles Villa-Vicencio

On Taking Responsibility

Why have I chosen to become involved in the Truth and Reconciliation Commission? The editors of this volume have asked me to reflect on the question. I begin with a story. In the latter part of the essay I suggest that the Commission presents the church and other faith communities with a challenge and a focused opportunity for ministry.

Taking Responsibility for the Past

My story involves a conversation that took place at the Gate of Death, leading to the Auschwitz 11 – Birkenau death camp in Poland. Behind us lay the terrible railway track leading to the crematoriums: a symbol of the death of six million Jews and a million other people. These included non-Jewish Poles, Rama (Gypsies), homosexuals, disabled people, Jehovah's Witnesses and other representatives of Hitler's *Untermensch*. "Tough, huh," observed Rainer Weizel, a German host. The holocaust is quite unique. No act of such magnitude can ever be relativised. It is also universal. It discloses the depths of human inhumanity. Gift Moerane, an activist and pastor from Thokosa township on the East Rand, was visibly moved by the visit: "Is this the last word – death?" The power of Auschwitz-Birkenau, the Warsaw Ghetto and so many other memorials in Europe commemorating Nazism is precisely their negativity. Death is death.

The memorials of death, the chauvinistic monuments of both

colonial and apartheid rule that glorify the arrogance of those who violated the rights of others in the past, and the countless memories of suffering and death that make up the history of South Africa are numerous. They too, speak of death. But that cannot be the last word. Our dealing with the past *must* open the gate to new life in the future.

We need to grasp the political resilience, the moral transcendence and the spiritual resources that permeate the depths of historical and contemporary despair. Some in the Warsaw Ghetto fought against the Nazi occupying force. There were underground activity, escapes, sabotage and rebellion in the death camps. South African history is permeated by resistance, struggle and hope. We must harness *this* memory, a memory which is part of the story of suffering – allowing *it* to shape our future.

If we fail to claim the human capacity to rise above the very worst that life can offer, we find ourselves wallowing in the morbidity of the past as an end in itself. It fails to become the phoenix from which a new society can rise. This is the challenge that faces the Truth and Reconciliation Commission in South Africa. The delicate balance between past suffering and future hope simply must be maintained. The stories of submission, surrender, defeat, death – and of hope and resistance – need to be remembered in order to create within the soul of the nation a commitment to a life in which the atrocities of the past will one day be no more than a sad and disturbing memory.

That, in brief, is why I (a Christian minister, a theologian and a social scientist) have chosen to work on the staff of the Truth and Reconciliation Commission! It is because I believe that if the Christian faith does not ultimately contribute to healing and reconciliation – which involves the difficult process of confession, repentance, reparation and forgiveness (and there are no short cuts!), the gospel is little more than celestial escapism.

The problem with the past is that it stubbornly refuses to go away of its own accord. It needs to be confronted – cautiously, carefully and sensitively, but also honestly, frankly and openly. Incorrectly or brashly faced it has the capacity to bleed the nation to death. It can unleash a cycle of violent revenge. Correctly and sensitively handled it can lead to a national catharsis, enabling the people of this land to lay the past to rest (without ever forgetting it), while drawing on the heroic spirit that overcame the structures of oppression in the creation of a new future.

In addressing a multi-faith service in St George's Cathedral in Cape Town, in which the Truth and Reconciliation commissioners were dedicated, President Mandela spoke of past guilt and suffering, while suggesting there is a sense in which we are all victims of apartheid. There is also a sense in which every South African needs to take responsibility for the past, acknowledging their guilt and committing themselves to the process of repentance and reparation.

The church and other religious organisations – whose unique task it is to evoke the spiritual resources of the nation in pursuit of liberating and healing ideals – has a special role in this regard. It is to invite every South African to discern just how the past has impacted on him or her, to accept his or her particular responsibility regarding the past and to resolve to do what reasonably needs to be done in the creation of a new future.

In 1946 Karl Jaspers (who, together with his Jewish wife, narrowly escaped deportation to a concentration camp) delivered a lecture at Heidelberg University, under the translated English title: *The Question of German Guilt*. He suggested there are four levels of guilt, all of which need to be propitiated. Firstly, *criminal guilt*. Its jurisdiction, he suggested, rested with the Nuremberg trials, before which some individual aggressors were to stand trial. Secondly, *political guilt*. This, he argued, extended beyond individual Nazi perpetrators. Only active resisters could claim exemption. All others were obliged to take political responsibility for the actions of the state. Thirdly, *moral guilt* (the personal or spiritual side of political complacency). This he saw as extending to everyone who "conveniently closed their eyes to events, or permitted themselves to be intoxicated, seduced or bought with personal advantages, or obeyed from fear." Finally, there is *metaphysical guilt*, which is a sense of *corporate guilt*, in which we all share by virtue of our common humanity. "Before God," suggests Jaspers, "it is not a case of some, or the majority, or many, or most, but *all* who are guilty."

Such acknowledgement prevents anyone from suggesting they are beyond the possibility of committing the gruesome and shameful acts of others. Dr Jósef Garlinski, in his book *Fighting*

Auschwitz, written as a memorial to the victims of Auschwitz, reminds us that the young SS men "could have been your sons or mine". They were brain-washed, trained to be brutal, to follow orders, coming to believe that to show human compassion or remorse was to be a bad German and a bad soldier. To recognise the potential for evil in all humanity, suggests Jaspers, is what makes possible "a new source of active life".

Martin Niemöller, a U-Boat commander in World War 1, who later became a Lutheran minister and leader of the Confessing Church, was imprisoned in Sachsenhausen and Dachau for opposing Nazism. He repeatedly sought to relate the crimes of the Nazi regime and the core moral guilt of the entire nation, without equating the two. "We should not blame the Nazis [alone] – they will find their prosecutors and judges, we should blame ourselves and draw logical conclusions." In South Africa, perpetrators will have the option of appearing before the Truth and Reconciliation Commission. Alternatively they risk being brought before the Courts. Politicians who may have sanctioned and authorised the gross human rights violations of others may well be confronted with the same options.

The Act governing the South African Truth and Reconciliation Commission at the same time emphasises the importance of disclosure of truth as the governing principle in requests for amnesty. Josè (Pepe) Zalaquett, a member of the Chilean National Commission on Truth and Reconciliation, argues that "truth is at least as important as justice". Reporting on the Argentinian situation, he suggests: "If the secrets of the 'dirty war' remain concealed from public opinion in Argentina, and also from soldiers never called to account for the horrors, then perhaps ... defendants and their accomplices will indeed be granted justification – not by history, but by the lack of it." Differently stated: To the extent that a people are allowed not to face the reality of the past, to that extent are they able to avoid taking responsibility for the past – allowing those moral and political structures that produced the past to be perpetuated in the future. To return to Jaspers. It is only by acknowledging our guilt (at different levels) for the events of the past that we begin to share in "renewing human existence". It is then that we are forced to "take ourselves seriously". We are compelled to rise above the "triviality of indifferent, mere living".

The wisdom of Jaspers's and Zalaquett's words have significance, of course, not only for those who will seek amnesty or have their day in court. It has equal significance for those who have repeatedly disclaimed responsibility for apartheid. The number of people who claim never to have supported apartheid is, of course, growing by the day! It is a difficult thing to find a self-confessed racist in this 'new' South Africa. Some are even tempted to say: "I never knew." There are others who can with some justification say: "I never supported apartheid." Jaspers's words are again apposite: "The guilt question is more than a question put to us by others. It is one we must put to ourselves."

It is here that the churches and other religious organisations have a particular role to play. It is, at the same time, a function that can only be exercised to the extent that the stories of victims and survivors are made known and heard – and not all these stories will be told or heard within the immediate future. In the long years after the Commission's work is done, stories too deep and too anguishing to be told now will still wait to be told. Religious and other healing organisations have a ministry here too. I offer brief comment on the parallel role to the Truth and Reconciliation Commission of such organisations. It is a role which will of necessity also have to be exercised beyond the life of the Commission.

National Repentance
Religious organisations face a spiritual responsibility to plumb the depths of South Africa's moral ruin. A culture that has generated racism, gender discrimination, economic deprivation, the horrors of apartheid and gross human rights violations of the kind that will emerge within the course of the Truth and Reconciliation Commission hearings, stands in need of fundamental renewal. It contains structures of oppression and habits of moral degradation that, unless confronted and healed, will perpetuate themselves and continue to produce people capable of evil.

It was not until October 1945, in the first post-war Synod of the Evangelical Church in Germany, that the matter of national repentance was seriously addressed. This resulted in the *Stuttgart Confession of Guilt*. It has been described as one of the most remarkable confessions of church history, primarily because it was people who had fought against Nazism and suffered its persecution who were confessing their guilt. The central sentence of the *Confession* reads: "We have caused immeasurable suffering in various countries and peoples. Even if we fought against the awful ideology of National Socialism, we accuse ourselves of not confessing more courageously, not praying more devotedly, not believing more cheerfully, and not loving more urgently." Ultimately, however, the *Stuttgart Confession* was not a confession of guilt by the German Christians – or the nation as a whole. It was a public declaration to members of the Ecumenical Movement present at the Stuttgart meeting by those who were most deeply engaged in the church struggle against Nazism. Important as this was, the *Confession* lacked specificity and it failed to mobilise the support of grassroots Christians. It was essentially the confession of a group of courageous leaders. Few understood its theological significance. The *Darmstadt Declaration of Guilt* followed in 1947. It was a more concrete statement – addressing the nature of corporate and moral guilt. It enjoyed the support of many within the Confessing Church, but again failed to attract the support of grassroots Christians in Germany.

The history of theological confession against apartheid in South Africa contains several contours, reaching a turning point in the World Alliance of Reformed Churches' (WARC) declaration on apartheid as a heresy – subsequently adopted by most member churches of the South African Council of Churches (SACC). The *Kairos Document* was published in 1985, stating that the affirmation of reconciliation was being widely abused in the church as a means to obviate the need for fundamental change. It called Christians to radical disengagement from the state and other forces of apartheid both within and outside of the church. Other statements followed, including the *Harare Declaration* (1985) which called for support for liberation movements fighting against the apartheid regime and the *Lusaka Statement* (1987) which went a step further in declaring the South African government to be illegitimate.

The unbanning of political organisations and the release of Nelson Mandela and other political prisoners in 1990 resulted in a different kind of church response to the apartheid state. This response included the statement of the Rustenburg Conference held in November 1990, which brought together the most representative gathering of churches ever in South Africa. The statement included a confession of guilt for the sins of apartheid. Also important is the revised position of the Dutch Reformed Church regarding their support for apartheid. In October of the following year (1991) the South African member churches of the WCC met in Cape Town, committing themselves to the eradication of apartheid and other forms of exploitation in South African society.

In pursuit of these goals, various churches have committed themselves to programmes of renewal and structural change. The Methodist Church of Southern Africa has, for example, adopted a programme entitled *Journey to a New Land.* The United Congregational Church continues to address the structural implications of the *Kairos Document* for renewal in church and state. The SACC has, in turn, established several task forces on renewal. Drawing on both Christian theological and African Traditional Religious resources, these include a programme on healing. Plans are being made for ecumenical services of confession and purification.

In brief, the South African church, not unlike the German church in the wake of World War ll, has recognised the need to acknowledge its complicity in apartheid and the need to rise above it. What it has not done is face the full theological and moral implications of the confession of guilt. To do so in a manner akin to the discussion generated by Jaspers could lay the foundation for national renewal. In the words of the *Kairos Document:* "This is a dangerous time because if this opportunity is missed and allowed to pass by, the loss for the Church, for the Gospel and for all the people of South Africa will be immeasurable."

For this to happen, careful co-ordination and planning will be required. The possibility of an inclusive, inter-religious, multi-cultural act of repentance and renewal should be investigated. An attempt should be made to include every denomination and every congregation in the country – those who have historically supported apartheid and those that have been part of the resistance process. Ultimately the shape and content of the Confession ought to reflect the creativity and values of the grassroots communities. Devoid of this the Confession will lack legitimacy.

Listening to Survivors

"If you cannot understand my story, you do not accept me as your neighbour," Ellen Kuzwayo once told me. "I am an African woman. I've tried to share my soul, my way of seeing things, the way I understand life. I hope you understand." We continued to speak at some length. "Africa is a place of story-telling," she continued. "We need more stories, never mind how painful the exercise might be. This is how we will learn to love one another. Stories help us to understand, to forgive and to see things through someone else's eyes."

It takes time for stories to be told. Important stories reveal the sacredness of life. They point to events that have hurt and healed, produced death and given life. These are not easy stories to tell. Reconciliation cannot be forced. True stories are rarely told to strangers. "It was not easy for me to write my story. It was not easy to tell my story to people who I did not know. Sometimes I do not fully understand it myself," Kuzwayo says. This is what makes the Truth and Reconciliation Commission's task of hearing stories of victims a strained, albeit necessary exercise. It is necessary to spring the trap that has prevented people from telling their stories and thus prevented them from being understood (Kuzwayo).

"Scream as loud as you want; no one will hear you," torture victims in apartheid jails were often told by tormentors who were confident that knowledge of their crimes would never go beyond the cell walls. The defeat of the apartheid regime offers the opportunity for the suppressed anguish of these victims to be heard. "Now there is a chance for the whole world to hear the victims scream," suggests Marlene Bosset, of the Cape Town-based Trauma Centre for Victims of Violence and Torture. People must be allowed to tell their stories. The nation is obliged to hear them. It is in the encounter of telling, hearing and understanding that the reconciliation process can begin.

The Truth and Reconciliation Commission has clearly defined political objectives and legal parameters. Ultimately, however, work of the Commission is a deeply spiritual, theological and moral endeavour. The suffering of some has been so great that perhaps only God can ultimately forgive. Forgiveness is at the same time an ingredient of human existence that cannot be easily dismissed without significant personal and communal cost. It is ultimately not the task nor is it the right of anyone to tell anyone else to forgive. It is the task of the church to enable those who continue to be burdened by memories of suffering and destruction to deal with those memories as part of the healing process. It is also part of the responsibility of the church to ensure that those responsible (whether as active perpetrators or dispassionate observers) hear those stories.

Realistic Hope
The high ideals of theology need always to be upheld as goals towards which society needs to strive. The biblical vision of God's impending reign on earth always stands in judgement of the highest achievements of society. This having been said, it is always necessary to begin the journey of renewal somewhere. It involves taking the first step on the road to renewal.

This requires the actual prevailing circumstances to be taken into account in the pursuit of this renewal. South Africa has undergone a *negotiated* settlement. Three words are likely to dominate the political scene in the immediate future: truth, reconciliation and justice. Truth can and must be pursued as the basis of renewal. Reconciliation needs to be the goal of the process. The state does not, however, have the power nor the right to forgive. It can only offer amnesty. Forgiveness is the prerogative of survivors. Justice is a more controversial concept. Some justice can emerge from the Truth and Reconciliation Commission. But not all justice. It will take grace and remarkable political will for the nation to accept this reality. The alternative would be extremely costly to all involved. It is unrealistic to expect too much from the Commission. It is realistic to hope that it will deliver something to the nation-building process.

BIBLIOGRAPHY
Jaspers, K. 1947. *Question of German Guilt* New York: Dial Press

Etienne de Villiers

The Challenge to the Afrikaans Churches

Introduction

In a letter, published in the official weekly of the Dutch Reformed Church (*Die Kerkbode*) of the 10th of February and signed by more than forty of its ministers, the Dutch Reformed Church (DRC) was challenged to support the Truth and Reconciliation Commission (TRC) more openly and constructively.

What is interesting about the letter is, above all, the fact that the ministers found it necessary to write it. At the time the General Synodical Commission ("ASK") of the DRC had already made several public statements about the TRC. In the statements reservations and warnings with regard to the possible derailment of the TRC prevailed. Although the statements did not denounce the TRC, no explicit support for it was expressed either. The authors of the letter clearly found such a tacit approach to the TRC and its task unsatisfactory.

I am of the opinion that the challenge openly and constructively to support the TRC, put by these ministers to the DRC, is indeed the greatest challenge with which the DRC, but also the other Afrikaans churches, is confronted with regard to the TRC.

Why All the Reservations?

Before I try to spell out why open and constructive support of the TRC by the Afrikaans churches is important, it is, first of all, necessary to get a clear picture of the reservations expressed about the TRC. In discussing the reservations I will restrict myself to the debate within the DRC with which I am acquainted. One can assume that most of these reservations were also voiced in other Afrikaans churches.

1. The most serious reservation, expressed in a statement by the General Synodical Commission of the DRC on the 19th of May 1995 and often repeated by representatives of the DRC, is that the TRC would not be impartial and would be determined in its proceedings by an ideological point of departure. An editorial in *Die Kerkbode* (26/5/95) refers to the statement by the Minister of Justice, Mr Dullah Omar, that offenses committed in defence of the apartheid regime are morally not on a par with offenses committed within the context of the liberation struggle. This statement, it is said, does not create the impression that the TRC will be impartial and without an ideological point of departure. In a discussion document on the TRC, prepared by the Committee for Doctrine and Current Affairs of the General Synod ("AKLAS") it is pointed out that if the TRC would deteriorate into something like the Nuremberg trials, and would brand only representatives of certain political parties as criminals, the process of reconciliation would not be served, but destroyed.

2. Another reservation, closely linked to the first one, is that the TRC would indeed not reduce the conflict in South Africa, but would rather increase it (Statement of 19 May). This would especially be the case if the TRC concentrates on offenses by representatives of the previous political regime, and ignores offenses by members of the liberation movement. It would also be the case if the ANC would use the TRC, or evidence uncovered by the TRC, to discredit other political parties and to further its own party political interests (Prof W D Jonker in *Die Kerkbode*, 28/7/95). There is, however, also the danger that the disclosure of the names of persons who committed serious human rights violations, could lead to acts of revenge by family members of the victims. For this reason, Prof Pieter Potgieter argues

that the disclosure of everything to everyone does not necessarily contribute to the good order in society (*Die Kerkbode*, 12/8/94).

3. A reservation, expressed not so much in official statements by the DRC, but by representatives of the DRC, is that the contextuality of truth would not be adequately taken into account by the TRC. Prof Danie du Toit, for example, points out that 200 years ago slavery was seen in quite a different light as today. Likewise, acts that today are seen as serious human rights violations, were 15 years ago regarded as absolutely necessary for the defence of the government against the "total onslaught" of the liberation movement and their communist allies. If offenses by representatives of the previous government are not seen against the background of the context in which they were perpetrated, the hearings of the TRC would not be fair (*Die Kerkbode*, 12/8/94).

4. The argument that reconciliation is primarily a moral and religious matter that cannot and should not be the objective of a legal instrument of the state such as the TRC, was first brought forward by Prof Adam Small. Some representatives of the DRC, however, seem to argue along the same line. Prof Pieter Potgieter, for example, is of the opinion that forgiveness and reparation is, first of all, a matter between the transgressor and God. It is, by implication, definitely not a matter for which the TRC is suited (*Die Kerkbode*, 12/8/94).

Apart from the specific reservations about the TRC voiced by representatives of the DRC we have discussed so far, there are also reservations of a more general and hidden nature. These are not reservations about the TRC as such, but reservations about support to policies of the present government by a church institution. We must take into account that the DRC has over the last decades been struggling to free itself from its ideological support for the apartheid policies of the Nationalist government. The detrimental effect of this support made the DRC leadership extremely cautious of again supporting government policies. To this caution the growing perception of many of the members of the DRC that the present government does not care for the interests of especially white Afrikaners, but in fact introduces policies, such as affirmative action, that harm them, also contributes. Much of the negative comment on the TRC, published in the Afrikaans press, only reflects this negative perception.

Why Positive Endorsement?
In the light of the reservations mentioned it is understandable that the DRC is hesitant to endorse openly and positively to the TRC. I am, however, of the opinion that the DRC – and other Afrikaans churches – should overcome this hesitancy. To put it even stronger: I am of the opinion that the Afrikaans churches have the calling not only critically to monitor the TRC and the way it operates, but also to play a more constructive and supportive role with regard to it. My reasons are the following:
1. *Critically to monitor the TRC is only part of the prophetic task of the church.* The DRC declared itself willing to take on the task of critically monitoring the proceedings of the TRC (Statement, 19/5/95). In this way it hopes to fulfil its prophetic task with regard to the TRC. I want to point out two problems with restricting the prophetic role of the DRC to a critical one. The first is the problem of credibility. Representatives of the present government will hardly find it credible if the DRC, which for so long supported the policies of the previous government, now suddenly – after the advent of the new political dispensation – has nothing but criticism to offer with regard to the policies of the new government. To them it will again smack of ideological bias on the part of the DRC.

More important, however, is the second problem. To criticise government policies which are in conflict with the church's interpretation of the Word of God, is only part of its prophetic task. The other part is to encourage and endorse government policies and developments in society which are in accordance with its understanding of the message of the Bible. As Christians we believe that God does not only work within the parameters of the church, but also in society and in nature. The horizons of his Kingdom are much wider than the borders of the church. God does not only use the church to further the cause of his Kingdom. He also uses institutions such as the state as his instruments. That the state is a servant of God, is also acknowledged by the DRC, inter alia in the 1990 report *Church and Society*: "It is the task and calling of the government, as servant of God, to ensure peace, rest and justice, and to care for the welfare of all its subjects" (par 290).

If God, in his common grace, uses the state to promote what is good in the world, the church cannot restrict its prophetic task to criticism of the policies of governments. It must also be willing positively to endorse government policies which ensure peace, rest and justice and which promote the welfare of all its subjects. Such endorsement of government policies will, of course, always have to be *conditional*, only in so far and as long as a particular policy reflects biblical principles. Support of a particular government policy will therefore always have to go hand in hand with criticism of those aspects of the policy which are not in accordance with biblical principles.

2. *The church should promote reconciliation not only within the domain of the church, but also in society.* Prof Pieter Potgieter correctly emphasises that reconciliation is primarily a religious matter between God and individual believers. He is, however, wrong in creating the impression that reconciliation between God and individual believers is the sole dimension of reconciliation in which the church is interested.

The peace that Jesus Christ brought about by reconciling us with God is of a comprehensive nature. To quote from the report on "The peace task of the church in South Africa" that was adopted at the General Synod of the DRC in 1990: "The peace that Jesus brings, is nothing less than the comprehensive *shalom* expected by the Old Testament. It should be realised in every dimension of human existence ... It comprises harmony and fulfilment in all the relationships of human beings. It relates to the individual and to the community, to the church and to society" (Agenda, pp 89 and 90; translated from Afrikaans).

As a result of the comprehensive nature of the peace that Christ brings, the church is not only interested in reconciliation between God and individual sinners, but also in reconciliation between conflicting individuals,

144

churches, classes, races, nations and countries. It is, to be more specific, also interested in reconciling those people who were victims of the apartheid policies with those who were responsible for the afflictions victims of the apartheid policies suffered. When institutions like the TRC are created to bring about this reconciliation the church cannot remain aloof and refuse to support such an institution. It should rather support such an institution and do everything it can to ensure that the objective of reconciliation is indeed achieved.

3. *The TRC is an imperfect, but suitable instrument to promote reconciliation.* It is quite possible to agree that reconciliation between those who formed part of the liberation movement and those who constituted and defended the apartheid regime, should be promoted by Christians, but nonetheless to argue that an institution such as the TRC is not a suitable one for bringing about this reconciliation. We have seen that many of the reservations representatives of the DRC have about the TRC are based on the assumption that it is not a suitable instrument for reconciliation.

One way to establish whether the TRC is a suitable instrument for reconciliation is to compare it with two alternative ways of handling serious human rights violations of the apartheid era. One alternative is to take the attitude of "ignore and forget" as point of departure. It is, in other words, for the Government to do absolutely nothing about the grievances of victims of serious human rights violations during the apartheid era in the hope that these grievances will eventually fade away. The bitterness over the plight of many women and children in concentration camps during the Second Boer War, which strained relations between English people and Afrikaners for many decades is, however, ample proof that such hope would be vain. The wounds inflicted during the apartheid era are in many cases of such a serious nature that they will not heal if left to themselves. They will only heal if they are properly treated.

The other alternative is to take the attitude of "punish and forget" as point of departure. This is an attitude that victims of serious human rights violations and/or their families often display. They want the perpetrators of serious human rights violations to be prosecuted and to pay for their deeds. The hard reality is, however, that this type of "Nuremberg trial" approach is only possible in situations where one of the adversaries gained a clear military victory and is in the position to enforce prosecution of the leaders of the defeated party. This is clearly not the case in South Africa. The transfer of political power in South Africa was the result of long and hard negotiations. The transfer of political power would not have been possible if the parties involved had not agreed that amnesty would, subject to certain conditions, be granted to all perpetrators of serious human rights violations incurred in the course of the military struggle between the Nationalist government and the liberation movement. Experience has shown, amongst others in Chile and Uruguay, that in negotiated transfers of political power, the only politically viable way to deal with the past is the establishment of something like the TRC.

Something like the Nuremberg trials would, however, not only be politically impossible in South Africa. One can also seriously question the appropriateness of such trials from an ethical point of view. The "victor's justice" that is executed in such trials is usually a one-sided justice which highlights the human rights violations of the defeated party and ignores those perpetrated by the victors. As a result of the fact that the "victor's justice" is experienced by the defeated party as one-sided and unfair such trials do not contribute to reconciliation but to renewed bitterness and strife.

In the case of an institution such as the TRC less emphasis is laid on "justice", which is in any case very difficult – if not impossible – to achieve in post-war situations. As the name indicates it is "truth and reconciliation" which are emphasised. A forum is created in which victims of serious human rights violations can describe and register what was done to them, can voice their bitterness and sorrow and can make enquiries about what happened to family members who had disappeared. Perpetrators get the opportunity to confess human rights violations without fear of prosecution and to provide information about what happened to people who had disappeared. The rationale is that the disclosure of truth will in itself have a liberating effect on both perpetrators and

146

victims. As reconciliation is only possible on the basis of the truth, it will hopefully also contribute to reconciliation between individuals and groups that were political enemies.

Of course, there is a chance that information gained at TRC hearings will enable someone to take revenge for the killing of a father or brother. It should be taken into account, however, that many victims and their families know exactly who the perpetrators are. The chances are even better that they will take personal revenge if absolutely nothing is done by the Government. If the TRC functions in a proper way it will act as a lightning conductor for strong and vengeful feelings and will prevent rather than encourage acts of personal revenge.

It should be clear from what has been said so far that the TRC cannot be compared to the Nuremberg trials. There is also very little chance that it will deteriorate into something like the Nuremberg trials, because it has a completely different point of departure and, in any case, does not have the legal power to punish anyone. Although there may be factions within some political parties that would like the TRC solely to concentrate on violations by representatives of the Nationalist government, the commissioners of the TRC are bound by law to be even-handed in their approach. Since the establishment of the TRC, the appointed chairperson, Archbishop Desmond Tutu, has more than once stressed the resolute intention of the TRC to be impartial. Of special importance is his renouncement of Min Dullah Omar's viewpoint that human rights violations perpetrated by representatives of the liberation movement should be treated differently. There is, in other words, at this stage little reason to believe that the TRC has an ideological point of departure and will be biased in its approach.

In contrast to some representatives of the DRC who fear that the contextuality of truth will not be adequately acknowledged by the TRC, I am of the opinion that it will rather contribute to a better understanding of the contextuality of truth. One of the roots of the misunderstanding and strife between different groups in South Africa is precisely the fact that they have for many years been caught up in different versions of the truth about South African society. During the eighties, for example, those who were in the camp of the Government believed that revolutionary violence, instigated by "terrorists" and their "communist allies", was responsible for all the violence in the country, and should be countered by a "total strategy". Those who were part of the liberation movement believed that the structural violence of apartheid and the reactionary violence of the security forces of the "apartheid regime" were the main causes of violence and should be countered by a "total onslaught". In both camps there were those who, more than others, believed that their viewpoint reflected the absolute truth about our society, and as a result, also believed that almost anything is permitted in the fight against the enemy.

There is only one way in which this belief in the absolute truth of the viewpoint of one's own group and the fanatical conduct that results from it, can be countered. Members of one's own group should be exposed to the viewpoints of other groups in South Africa and vice versa. It is not only in confronting the viewpoints of other groups in debate that one becomes aware of the relativity of the truth of one's own viewpoint and is willing to correct and change it. It is even more the case when one has the opportunity to listen to the stories of the life experiences and suffering of members of other groups. Fortunately the exposure to the life stories of people from other groups has become a more frequent experience in South Africa during the last few years. The TRC offers another, crucial opportunity to share even those stories about bitter experiences that are difficult to tell, but need to be told in order to let the processes of inner healing and reconciliation take its course: stories of being victimised or of complicity in the victimisation of others.

4. *The DRC has already confessed its own guilt in supporting apartheid. It should therefore also encourage members to confess their sins of the apartheid past.* At the Rustenburg Church Conference in 1991 Prof Willie Jonker made his now famous confession for the wrongs of apartheid on behalf of the DRC and the Afrikaans people as a whole. He added: "I have the liberty to do just that, because the DRC at its latest synod has declared apartheid a sin and confessed its own guilt of negligence in not warning against it and distancing

itself from it long ago" (Alberts and Chikane 1991:92). Indeed, at the General Synod of 1990 the DRC adopted a revised version of the report *Church and Society* in which it for the first time in unequivocal terms admitted the ideological and racist nature of apartheid and confessed that it had adopted a too uncritical attitude towards it. It also admitted that it "had made the error of allowing forced separation and division of peoples in its own circle, to be considered a biblical imperative" (par 282 and 283).

In the light of its own confession of guilt the DRC does not only have the right, but also the moral obligation, to encourage members to confess sins committed in the pursuit of political ideals. This conclusion is also drawn in the above named discussion document of the Commission for Doctrine and Current Affairs of the General Synod on the TRC: "... the church should feel free to encourage all involved not only to confess sins of the apartheid past, but also sins committed in the struggle against apartheid. It is necessary that the country meets the future with a common will to forgive each other, to accept each other, to seek what is best for everyone and to walk the road to justice. With this in mind the church should encourage all people, whatever their political and religious affiliations may be, to make a new beginning as individuals and as community and to set the goal not to repeat the sins of the past" (p 4).

In the case of the DRC and other Afrikaans churches the church members that will need encouragement to confess their sins and to appear before the TRC will be predominantly members of the security forces during the apartheid era. Ministers of these churches will, in this regard, have to give guidance to at least three categories of church members:
(a) Members who are not sure whether they have anything to confess. Some members may, for example, wonder whether a serious human rights violation they had committed in the line of duty as part and parcel of the "total strategy" of the security forces should be called a sin and should be confessed. Ministers will have to help them understand that the killing or torture of a fellow human being involves personal guilt whatever the circumstances are.

(b) Members who acknowledge their sins and are willing to confess it, but are not sure whether they should also ask to appear before the TRC. Ministers will have to indicate to them that the confession of guilt is not only a private matter between the believer and God, but also a "public" matter between the sinner and all those people that suffered as a result of his or her sin. A forum that enables such a meeting between violator and victim should be made use of.

(c) Members who acknowledge their sins and are willing to confess, but cannot understand why they, who executed serious human rigths violations, should take all the blame and appear before the TRC, whilst others, who were involved in encouraging and even planning such violations, are not accused. Apart from pointing out that everyone should take responsibility for his or her own sins, whether others are willing to do so or not, ministers can also draw attention to the motive of substitution which plays such a central role in Christian belief. By vicariously bearing the responsibility for a serious human rights violation in which other people were also involved, by vicariously confessing guilt and appearing before the TRC also on behalf of others, one can contribute to a process of reconciliation and healing which benefits also those others involved and even society at large.

5. *The DRC has an important role of pastoral support to play to members who are called to appear before the TRC.* This is a fact that is acknowledged by the leaders of the DRC. In its statement on the TRC of the 19 May 1995 the executive committee of the General Synodical Commission "strongly appealed to church councils and ministers to provide pastoral guidance to those who become involved in the process either as victims or accused".

One may assume that in the case of the DRC and other Afrikaans churches it will predominantly be church members who are accused of serious human rights violations that will appear before the TRC. These members will indeed need intensive pastoral care: from the moment that they receive a summons to appear until long after the whole process has been completed. It is a serious question whether all local church councils and ministers are in a position to provide the specialised and intensive pastoral care that will be needed. Its seems to me that the DRC – and other Afrikaans churches – should do more than to just appeal to church councils and ministers to provide the necessary pastoral guidance. They should preferably, on a regional basis, appoint special counsellers for church members who are summoned to appear before the TRC.

6. *The TRC will only function successfully if the DRC and other Afrikaans churches lend it their support.* Afrikaners in general are in the peculiar position in the present South African society that they have far less control over political, legal and other insitutions than a few years ago. Nonetheless, many of these institutions still cannot function properly without the co-operation and support of Afrikaners. It is, for example, the case with the civil service where the expertise of Afrikaans-speaking officials are still needed. It is also the case with the TRC. If the political parties of the Afrikaner, the Afrikaans newspapers and, in particular, the Afrikaans churches withdraw their support and encourage Afrikaners to refuse any co-operation with the TRC, the TRC will surely not succeed in achieving its objectives. The failure of the TRC – especially if it can be blamed on the Afrikaners and their institutions – will, however, have catastrophic consequences for peace and stability in the South African society.

While the opposition to, or even lack of support of the Afrikaans churches, can have dire consequences for the TRC and South African society, the constructive co-operation of these churches can do much to keep the TRC on track. The members of the TRC know that they need the co-operation of the Afrikaans churches and would therefore be cautious not to alienate them by, for example, operating in an ideological and biased manner.

Conclusion

As with so many other things in life we do not have any absolute guarantee that the TRC will indeed achieve the positive objectives it has been established for. It remains an imperfect institution which tries to deal with the past and promote reconciliation in our society by treading the middle ground between the two extremes of ignoring the past and punishing people for political wrongs of the past.

What we can be sure of, however, is that the churches – and that includes the Afrikaans churches – may not oppose the TRC or even withhold their support from it. The Afrikaans churches too have the responsibility to support the TRC and by constructive co-operation and criticism contribute to its success. For much more is at stake than just the failure or success of a particular government institution. What is at stake is whether the wounds of our apartheid past will be healed or will rather, for decades to come, remain a painful and disrupting reality in our society.

BIBLIOGRAPHY

AKLAS 1995. "Die Kommissie vir Waarheid en Versoening van die SA Regering" (Unpublished report)

Alberts, L. & Chikane, F. 1991. *The Road to Rustenburg. The Church Looking Forward to a New South Africa*. Cape Town: Struik Christian Books

Boraine, A. Levy, J. & Scheffer, R. 1994. *Dealing with The Past. Truth and Reconciliation in South Africa*. Cape Town: Idasa

Bronkhorst, D. 1995. *Truth and Reconciliation. Obstacles and Opportunities for Human Rights*. Amsterdam: Amnesty International Dutch Section

De Gruchy, J. W. 1993. "Guilt, Amnesty and National Reconstruction", *Journal of Theology for Southern Africa* no 83, 3-13

De Gruchy, J. W. 1994. "Review article: Forgetting or Exorcising the Past?", *South African Outlook* vol 124 no 6, 63-65

Dutch Reformed Church 1990. *Church and Society*. Bloemfontein: General Synodical Commission

Du Toit, A. 1994. "Laying the Past to Rest", *Indicator SA* vol 11 no 4, 63-69

Smit, D. J. 1995. "The Truth and Reconciliation Commission – Tentative Religious and Theological Perspectives", *Journal of Theology for Southern Africa* no 90, 3-15

South African Council of Churches 1989. *Confessing Guilt in South Africa. The Responsibility of Churches and Individual Christians.* Johannesburg: SACC

H Russel Botman

Pastoral Care and Counselling in Truth and Reconciliation: Types and Forms of Pastoral Work

Our sons and our daughters are facing a different and new future. Our preconceptions and our natural lines of communication are being tested as a new nation is being born. Our knowledge and our pastoral skills are fundamentally challenged by this new reality. We need, therefore, to reconsider the questions of types and forms of pastoral care in the life of a nation in search of its past in order to build its future. This chapter therefore considers options for pastoral care responsibility in the context of the truth and reconciliation process.

This challenge is enormous. We are called upon not merely to do an audit of existing types and forms of pastoral action. We are challenged with a reality so fundamentally new that existing forms of pastoral action require revisitation and transformation. Such new forms cannot be developed in any one area of the country alone, or even worse, in any one pastoral care and counselling centre. It requires an ecumenical and corporate process if we really mean to serve the rainbow nation in a way that will not only heal individuals but actually take a nation from division to unity, from fear and violence to community and liberation.

This article is based on a paper originally delivered as the Keynote Address at the Conference of The Southern African Association for Pastoral Work, 9-11 May 1995. A different version of the paper was published in *The Journal of Pastoral Ministry*, No 7, July 1995.

Research done at the University of Chicago indicates that when change takes place four sectors are formed within a society. Ten percent of the people are usually the innovators in the process. Forty percent are fast adaptors, while another forty percent can be described as slow adaptors. The final ten percent, the laggards, lag behind the process significantly. These differences in the community complicate the pastoral challenge of the rainbow people. The situation is made significantly worse in this context because of the fact that each of these sectors are made up of both victims and perpetrators. Such a community suffers a double jeopardy. The issue is further complicated by the fact that people have been forcefully divided by apartheid's laws over several decades, and continue to be divided by the ongoing economic divisions in the society.

We cannot merely transpose American or European solutions in the search for new pastoral forms to address the unique situation we are faced with. We need a process – a shared, multicultural, community based, nonsexist and nonracial, provincially co-ordinated programme of pastoral care development. The answer to our question lies somewhere within this changing community. A refreshingly new pastoral process is in fact taking place in many communities across the country. We clearly need to participate creatively in this process. The question is, where shall we start?

A Legal or Pastoral Symbol?
At present all the roads of new beginnings in South Africa seem to lead through the Truth and Reconciliation Commission.

In analysing the response of the Churches to the TRC, I refer to formal responses to the Commission put forward by three bodies: The Research Institute on Christianity in South Africa (RICSA) at the University of Cape Town, the theological faculty of the University of the Western Cape, and the statement of the Church Leaders under the banner of the South African Council of Churches. The consensus of these responses is that the TRC is an important *national symbol* that relates in crucial ways to the practice of pastoral care.

RICSA describes the TRC as a national care process. "It will show that the nation cares." Its point of departure is that all the people of South Africa have suffered irreparably from the history of this country. As such the TRC has a pastoral function with regard to the perpetrators as well as the victims. The grand motive for this pastoral action process is the restoration of the people's humanity. As a symbol the Commission is described as "a public liturgical act which could focus the purgation of feelings and ... signal a pledge to make a new beginning". The memorandum reminds one of a statement made by Charles Villa-Vicencio: "Perhaps the most important contribution that religion can realistically make as the country struggles to find new direction, is the promotion of a sense of a national catharsis. It is to assist the nation to 'put the lights on' and to admit the extent to which it has violated the humanity of its people. It is to enable the nation to turn away from the past to a fundamentally different kind of future" (1993).

The Church Leaders Consultation of the SACC agrees that the TRC is a national symbol. They differ from the UCT viewpoint in that they do not see the Commission as a symbol of care. They see the Commission as *a legal symbol* on which pastoral action can, nevertheless, capitalise. The central pastoral aim is described as "making our memories redemptive": "We as the religious community take a separate but parallel responsibility to the commission ... before, during and after this process ... to make our memories redemptive ..."

They then declare that the pastoral function belongs by nature to the church. Consequently five stages of pastoral action proper in which the religious community should be involved are identified:

1. Helping the nation to come to terms with the past as well as to move from the old to the new;
2. providing for counselling and confession, or predisclosure guidance or counselling;
3. offering a ministry of accompaniment of the confessant to the room of confession, in this case the Truth Commission;
4. effecting the priestly liturgical function of atonement to help the nation to accept the reality of the past and develop corrective measures to ensure that those experiences are never repeated;
5. accompanying the nation into a new life, a new experience, a new culture, and a new morality.

The response of a number of theologians at the University of the Western Cape supports the position of the Church Leaders on the proper and separate responsibility of pastoral care . Yes, the TRC is a national legal symbol. They go even further to identify a narrow legal focus, namely the contravention of human rights. However, the church's responsibility, they maintain, goes beyond the concern for the contravention of human rights by individuals. The church is *pastorally* concerned about truth and reconciliation. As such, they argue, the church would understand that the government has to close the human rights book on the past. But the pastoral care book cannot be closed.

Areas of Concern
The primary area of concern has to do with the intent of the process of truth-seeking, namely to find healing and reconciliation. Clinebell aptly states that pastoral counselling consists of the establishment and the subsequent utilisation of a relationship; the quality of which can be described as *therapeutic* (healing), *maieutic* (facilitating birth and growth) and *reconciling* (restoring alienated relationships)" (1984: 74).

There is indeed a group of significant theologians in South Africa who argue that the process should be "about the truth and nothing but the truth", i.e. that truth and not reconciliation should be the primary concern of the process. Their point of departure is that the commission is a legal and political instrument. It will investigate a crime against humanity. A further point of departure for the investigation must be the biblical preferential option for the victims of apartheid and colonialism. This calls for a moral and legal separation of those who suffered under apartheid and colonialism and those who supported it. A legal equilateral treatment of opposing forces and supporters of apartheid will lead to a distortion of historical facts.

Although it would be important to give the latter viewpoint its due regard, the legal and political reality already dictates a reconciliatory truth-seeking process. This may be the price we have to pay for the kind of transition we had to negotiate, for letting the sun set on the standoff between victim and perpetrator.

157

The situation we are facing is clearly a national catharsis. The church and pastoral care workers have no other option but to put a significant programme of pastoral action in place to respond to this envisaged national catharsis.

I now wish to point to some of the main areas of pastoral concern around the issue of the "truth and reconciliation seeking".

Truth and *reconciliation*

Kistner correctly reminds us in an article which appears elsewhere in this volume, that the Pauline word "reconciliation" indicates wholeness and healing, and is therefore close to the Hebrew "shalom". At the time of Paul the word "reconciliation" was mostly used to describe the act of humanity to restore community and communication between enemies. The crux of the matter, Kistner maintains, is that the centrality of the notion of reconciliation in the church implies two things: (a) the church is an alternative society, and (b) the church is obliged to struggle against all structures and practices of irreconcilability in its own life as well as in society. The chief pastoral concern of the church in dealing with the Truth, he says, is the task of "healing the wounds" and the creation of community.

He then continues to make two poignant observations regarding the practice of pastoral action:
1. Churches should devote great care towards facilitating opportunities for encounter and fellowship between the perpetrators and the victims of oppression during the apartheid regime and assist them to exchange their stories and experiences and fears with the view to a process of mutual acceptance and forgiveness.
2. The society and the religious or ideological community or cultural group which has contributed towards shaping the mind of the offender shares in the responsibility of the offence and is in need of repentance on its part and forgiveness on the part of God and the victims with the view to facilitating a process of healing and taking precautions against a repetition of the offence.

With these remarks Kistner pictures the scene of the Truth and Reconciliation Commission as a pastoral care concern focusing on reconciliation. Pastoral care of the encounter group type is the essential strategy and storytelling its nature. But, warns Robert Schreiter (1992), the risk of falling into the trap of a false reconciliation is also at stake.

Schreiter identifies three types of false reconciliation: (a) reconciliation as a hasty peace; (b) reconciliation that does not lead to liberation; (c) reconciliation as a managed process. To avoid the first pitfall we need the TRC. To steer away from a false reconciliation that does not lead to liberation of the oppressed we need the Reconstruction and Development Programme. In order to avoid the last form of false reconciliation – i.e. reconciliation that manifests as life-long management of conflict – we also need a focused pastoral care programme including traditionally Western and traditionally African forms.

Transforming Pastoral Care Types

Concerned people in the Western Cape have established a religious forum for the Truth and Reconciliation process. This forum has subcommittees responsible for lobbying the Government, for educating the public, for fundraising, and also for pastoral counselling of the victims and the perpetrators. Pastoral workshops involving the victims have been held and more are planned throughout the process.

A particular world-view and understanding of how the church relates to the broader society determines the way in which we identify and define different types and forms of pastoral action.

These developments in the Western Cape led me to think of Community Forum Pastoral Action as one of the contextual forms of pastoral care. Community Forum based Pastoral Care has the capacity to unite or combine all types and forms of pastoral care, pastoral counselling, therapy and community care programmatically in pastoral action. Organised as a religious forum, such a Pastoral Forum takes for granted that pastoral action is primarily the responsibility of the religious community. More than that, it assumes that the pastoral action is driven by people of faith. It seeks to relocate pastoral action within caring communities. Pastoral care is now challenged with demythologising and demystifying its work and becoming more accessible to the community. Its primary location should be the caring community.

I want to argue further that we are now facing the challenge of a significant shift in pastoral care. Pastoral care must move away from its traditional world-view and must revisit its underlying concept of how the church relates to a society in transition. A society in transition calls pastoral care into the open Community Forum where it has to go beyond the mission and evangelism bias (both which are based on a particular construction of the relationship between the church and the society) to the Forum Care process (caring with the community as a religious community).

I call this a necessary distinction because I do not regard it as an extinction of our Christian identity. Neither do I see in these a life-threatening crisis between professionals in pastoral care and the activities of the caring community. It is the empowerment of the caring community for its own pastoral care work that is presently at stake.

Seeking new forms is also a treacherous terrain. At the end of the Second World War Europeans introduced a new form of pastoral care in their work, namely Clinical Pastoral Formation. They imported this innovation from the USA. This innovation met with huge resistance in Europe. A main reason given for the resistance was that the new pastoral form tended to cause the loss of the primary place of theology in pastoral care and, secondly, that its practical implication was to provide pastoral care in a form that stabilises the status quo instead of prophetically challenging it.

Narrative as Pastoral Action

I am attracted to the use of storytelling in pastoral action. In this regard I am in full agreement with Kistner's suggestion. This is a most challenging project which also empowers the victims.

Apartheid was a crime against humanity. It was constructed to destroy the human identity of black people. An identity is given by God and preserved in stories or narratives. These stories are our memories. Therefore, Schreiter correctly concludes: "To trivialize and ignore memory is to trivialize and ignore human identity, and to trivialize and ignore human identity is to trivialize and ignore human dignity" (1992: 19).

He then begins to explain that the political violence of apartheid was an attempt "to destroy the narratives that sustain

160

people's identities and substitute narratives of its own" (1992: 34). He calls the latter "narratives of the lie", narratives of negation. The negation was not only meant to destroy the narrative of the victim, but to pave the way for the oppressor's narrative. However, human beings cannot survive without narratives. In fact they survive through their memories wrapped up in stories. Their healing comes from narratives. Schreiter warns us: "The reconstruction of memory, however, is not simply a retrieval of memory. That old memory becomes so associated with violence that it becomes too painful to evoke. What must be done to overcome this suffering is to disengage the older memory from those acts of violence. That is done by repeating the narrative of the violence over and over again to ease the burden of trauma that it carries. Such an activity begins to put a boundary around the violence, as it were, to separate it from the memory. The tentacles of the lie burrow deep into memory, however, and extracting them does damage to the whole memory. For that reason memory must be reconstructed. It will never be the same again; it will bear the scars of its history" (1992: 38).

To deal with our past pastorally we need "to make our memories redemptive". Without memory we'll have no freedom. Without redeemed memories we'll have no future as a nation. Both our liberation and future require that we relinquish every natural-order or deterministic approach to memory to embrace a socio-theological constructionist approach in pastoral care.

We will have to search in the direction of the pioneering work of scholars such as Dieter Hessel (pastoral care as a social ministry), Howard Clinebell (holistic liberation-growth model of pastoral care and counselling), Stephen Pattison (pastoral care and political commitment), Don Browning (moral context of pastoral care), Holland and Henriot (social analysis as a tool of pastoral care), Alistair Campbell (the wounded healer), David Augsburg (cross-cultural pastoral care), and, closer to home, the work of Cochrane, de Gruchy and Petersen in *In Word and Deed: Towards a Practical Theology for Social Transformation* (pastoral care as transformation), Vivian Msomi (pastoral work from a grassroots African commitment), Denise Ackermann (a feminist pastoral care), J A Nxumalo (engaging the African world-view), Albert Nolan (pastoral work and social reconstruction), etc.

We must secure the empowerment of victims in pastoral work. It is so important that the victims are agents of the reconstruction of their memories and not the objects of some psycho-pastoral or missionary zeal. Especially those who were trained through a missionary theology that regarded those who were (are) the victims of apartheid as the missionary field or the vineyard for their toils must understand the nature of this kairos moment. This is the key to our future. The wounded are the healers. This is the biblical nature of reconciliation. The wounded are not the object of healing, but the subject thereof. This is the way of Jesus Christ, the Truth and the Life.

BIBLIOGRAPHY

Clinebell, H. 1984. *Basic Types of Pastoral Care and Counseling.* Parthenon: Nashville

Kistner, W. 1994. *The Legacy of the Past in the New South Africa.* Stellenbosch: EFSA

Schreiter, R. 1992. *Reconciliation: Mission and Ministry in a Changing Social Order.* New York: Orbis.

Villa-Vicencio, C. 1993. "Keeping the Revolution Human: Religion and Reconstruction" *JSR No 6*, Vol 2, September

APPENDIX

A SERVICE OF DEDICATION AND BLESSING OF COMMISSIONERS OF THE TRUTH AND RECONCILIATION COMMISSION

"I invite you to join in the search for truth without which
there can be no genuine reconciliation."

Mr Dullah Omar – Minister of Justice

**ST GEORGE'S CATHEDRAL
CAPE TOWN
13 FEBRUARY 1996
1:00pm**

ORDER OF SERVICE

- The Procession of participants in the service:
- Welcome and intention of service
- Song : We Shall Overcome

(During this song the **Minister of Justice** will light the Candle of Peace)

We shall overcome
We shall overcome
We shall overcome some day
Oh, deep in my heart, I do believe
We shall overcome some day
We'll walk hand in hand
We'll walk hand in hand
We'll walk hand in hand some day
Oh, deep in my heart, I do believe
We shall overcome some day

The truth will set us free
The truth will set us free
The truth will set us free some day
Oh, deep in my heart, I do believe
We shall overcome some day

The Call to Prayer:

from the Moslem community

from the Jewish community

Litany (The congregation is invited to respond):

Don't accept anything simply because it has been said by your teacher,
or it has been written in your sacred book
or it has been believed by many
or it has been handed down by your ancestors.

Accept and live according to
what will enable you to see the truth face to face

166

Creator God
We repent what has happened in our land.
We mourn the opportunity squandered and
the suffering of people.
We repent the loss of precious human lives,
the torture maiming and killing of our children.
We mourn the loss of human dignity and worth.

Lord in your mercy
Hear our prayer/Yiva umthandazo/Hoor ons gebed

In angs en met skaamte
bring ons die pole in ons samelewing voor u
onderdrukker en onderdrukte, slagoffer en oortreder,
en ons bid vir 'n einde aan die
vervreemding, vir genesing en herstel.

Lord in your mercy
Hear our prayer/Yiva umthandazo/Hoor ons gebed

Almighty One
We acknowledge that others have caused us to be bitter,
made us feel inferior, and deceived us.
We were never accepted,
our opportunity in life was removed.

We pray for compassion
We ask for peace/Sicela ukuba kube ko uxolol/Ons vra vir vrede

Ons het in ons kinders se oë gekyk en was oorweldig.
Ons het in ons ouers se oë gekyk en was teleurgestel.
Ons het in mekaar se oë gekyk en het weggedraai.

Ons bid vir meegevoel.
We ask for peace/Sicela ukuba kube ko uxolo/Ons vra vir vrede

Genadige God
Ons erken dat ons nooit geglo het wat gebeur het nie,
ons het die werklikheid probeer ontvlug,
ons het nooit werklik geluister of gehoor nie, ons het toegelaat
dat daar 'n wig tussen ons ingedryf word.
Vergewe ons.

Ons bid vir vergifnis.
Mercifully hear us/Ngetarhu sive/Hoor ons in genade

In your compassion touch each one of us
Heal the scars so we can touch one another
Support our tentative moves
to reach past our individual pain
to the hope of wholeness.

We pray for forgiveness
Mercifully hear us/Ngetarhu sive/Hoor ons in genade
From the darkest days to human liberty
From the darkest days to victory

We praise and thank God for new beginnings
and the promise of hope that lies ahead

There is no future without the past.
There is no day without the beginning.

Amen.

Readings and Sayings from sacred texts:

Led by members of the

Buddhist community
Christian community
Moslem community

Concluded by a Meditation and time of silence

THE ADDRESS:

President Nelson Mandela

THE DEDICATION AND BLESSING OF COMMISSIONERS

Each commissioner, *when* called by *name,* moves *forward and* receives a candle and olive *branch.* Each candle *is then lit from* the *peace* candle *and* the commissioners *stand in* a semi-circle, facing the congregation.

THE COMMISSIONERS

Desmond Tutu
Alex Boraine

Mary Burton
Chris de Jager
B B Finca
Sisi Khampepe
Richard Lyster
Wynand Malan
Khoza Mgojo
Hlengiwe Mkhize
Dumisa Ntsebeza
Wendy Orr
Denzil Potgieter
Mapule Ramashala
Mohamed Randera
Yasmin Sooka
Glenda Wildschut

The words of the dedication are read

We call upon you who have been appointed as
commissioners of the Truth and Reconciliation Commission
to acknowledge and recognise
as a sacred trust
the awesome responsibility that has been given to you.

We pledge you our support
and give you our blessing
in the task that lies before you.
and we ask that,
in your work for truth and reconciliation
you will be guided by
a wisdom greater than your own,
a Wisdom that knows and encompasses all truth.

Will you dedicate yourselves
to carry out the task
that has been entrusted to you
with the highest integrity, with impartiality
and compassion for all,
for the purpose of healing our nation?

The Commissioners *respond*: I WILL

The *Congregation* proclaims:

Go forward, in the light of truth, with our blessing.

The Commissioners remain on the platform to be blessed by *the faith communities followed by a* song.

The Commission Chairperson replies.

The National Anthem

This service was compiled and led by members of the communities of faith in the Western Cape, including:

Mr Louis du Plooy – Religious Response to the Truth and Reconciliation Commission
Mr Barney Beck – The Quaker Peace Centre
Imam G Solomon – The Muslim Judicial Council
Rabbi David Hoffman – Temple Israel
Rabbi Daman Kapplan – Temple Israel
Ms Patricia Van Stavel – The Brahma Kamaris World Spiritual University
Ms Tratiba Daya – The Brahma Kamaris World Spiritual University
Ms Rose de la Hunt – The Wellstead
Mr Rob Nairn – The Buddhist Community
Cannon Rowan Smith – St George's Cathedral
Bishop James Gribbel – The Methodist Church of SA
Dr Philip Kubukeli – Traditional Healers Association
Fr Peter-John Pearson – The Justice and Peace Department, Roman Catholic Church
Fr Christopher Ahrends – St George's Cathedral
Mr Edward Esau – St George's Cathedral

The Luthlaza High School Choir led by Lubbe Nyamende
The Astra School Choir led by Sharon Potgieter and Faried Swartz
The Western Cape Blind Association led by Evelyn Siwa and Patrick Bomela

Cathedral organist: Mr Grant Brasler
Music & Choirs arranged and led by Alvon Collison

Soloists: Welcome Witbooi and Francesca Blasich

Dedication read by Carmen Esau.

Notes on Contributors

Dr H Russel Botman
Senior Lecturer in Christianity and Society, University of the Western Cape. He currently is President of the Southern Africa Alliance of Reformed Churces. He has a D.Th degree from UWC. He also participates in the Religious Response to the Truth and Reconciliation Commission in the Western Cape.

Dr Robin M Petersen
Senior Lecturer in Christian Studies, University of the Western Cape. He has a MA degree from Cape Town, and a Ph.D from the University of Chicago.

Prof Denise Ackermann
Professor of Practical Theology at the University of the Western Cape. Prof. Ackermann is regarded as one of South Africa's leading feminist theologians, and has published widely in this and other fields.

Dr Willa Boesak
Senior Lecturer in Christianity and Society, University of the Western Cape. A Ph.D graduate from the University of Cape Town, his recently published book, *God's Wrathful Children* (Eerdmans 1995) has received wide acclaim.

Prof Etienne de Villiers
Professor of Ethics at the University of Pretoria. Prominent

expert on ethics and the life and work of the Dutch Reformed Church in S.A.

Terry Dowdall
Clinical psychologist, senior lecturer at the Child Guidance Clinic, University of Cape Town and Board member and consultant to the Trauma Centre for Victims of Violence and Torture.

Dr Cornel du Toit
Head of the Research Institute for Theology and Religion, University of South Africa.

Dr Wolfram Kistner
Director of Ecumenical Advice Bureau, and former Director of Research, South African Council of Churches.

Fr Michael Lapsley
Chaplain and Director, Trauma Centre for the Victims of Violence and Torture, Cape Town.

Min Dullah Omar
Minister of Justice, South Africa. Min Omar is an advocate by profession.

Prof Dirkie Smit
Professor of Christian Studies, University of the Western Cape. Prof Smit has published widely on Christian theology and issues of concern for the churches in South Africa.

Dr Molefe Tsele
Director of ESSET, a programme of the South African Council of Churches to provide analyses on economic and ethical issues for the churches.

Prof Charles Villa-Vicencio
Director of Research, Truth and Reconciliation Commission. Professor of Christian Studies at the University of Cape Town, and widely published theologian and ethicist.